The Handbook for Legal Leadership Success

GREAT **LAWYER** TO GREAT *leader*

HOW **LEADING LAWYERS** EMBRACE **COLLABORATION**, IGNITE **PASSION** AND INSPIRE **PERFORMANCE.**

MIDJA FISHER

Copyright © Melinda Fisher 2019

ISBN 978-0-6482946-1-0

Cover design, internal design and editing: Lauren Shay – Full Stop Writing, Editing and Design.

To My Fellow Lawyers.

About Midja

Midja Fisher is a leadership expert who inspires people to gain greater self-awareness and self-belief to lead with purpose, confidence and authenticity. She is a dynamic speaker, mentor and facilitator who shares her personal and professional stories openly and passionately.

Midja is a lawyer and former partner of Shine Lawyers, an ASX-listed company and one of Australia's largest compensation law firms. Midja began her career as an IT consultant for PricewaterhouseCoopers, before practising law and finding her passion in the field of learning and development. During her career, Midja has developed and facilitated a range of learning programs, from webinar series and induction programs to corporate workshops and six-day residential leadership retreats.

Midja specialises in the areas of authentic leadership, career confidence, company culture and values, and professional women's

ABOUT MIDJA

mentoring programs. She has worked with organisations such as the Toyota North Queensland Cowboys, SAP, Queensland Law Society, WSP, RSL Queensland, Australian Trade College and the Australasian Legal Practice Management Association (ALPMA). Midja was also nominated in the Telstra Business Women's Awards in 2017.

Midja's previous book, *Confidence – How to Be Your Most Authentic, Courageous and Unshakeable Self*, is a handbook for female leaders who want to increase their influence and take the next step in their careers. It provides a framework to help women gain the confidence to take their seat at the leadership table.

What's unique about Midja is her infectious energy, enthusiasm and optimism, which are evident in her work and personal life. Midja partners with individuals and organisations to create leaders people want to follow, teams people want to play with and organisations people want to belong to.

Midja lives on the Gold Coast and is a self-confessed sun worshipper, champagne drinker, hip-hop dancer and lover of life!

You can get in touch with Midja at www.midja.com.au.

Acknowledgements

I'm extremely grateful for those who have believed in me and inspired me throughout my life and career. I've always felt surrounded by a warm hug of love and support. What a wonderful way to live.

First, to those closest to me, my kids, Tom, Sophie and Jack, and my sister Rell, who I love unconditionally and who put up with all my craziness. You inspire me every day to dream big and pursue my lofty goals.

To the leading lawyers who have had the greatest influence on my career. Thank you for always giving me the opportunity to grow and learn and letting me just be me.

To my mentor, Jane Anderson, and the Women with Influence tribe. Your inspiration, support and honesty have made this a ride to remember. Thank you for sharing this time in my life. You keep

ACKNOWLEDGEMENTS

my head in the game and continue to push me out of my comfort zone. Love to you all!

To my editing and publishing team, Lauren Shay and Sylvie Blair. Thank you for your time, dedication and attention to detail. I look forward to us working together on the next book.

And to you, the reader and my fellow lawyer, thank you for picking up this book and committing to leading the legal profession into an exciting future.

Midja x

CONTENTS

INTRODUCTION

Introduction

31st January, 2000: my admission date as a solicitor. I fondly remember this momentous day, as I'm sure all lawyers do. It was a day of celebration. I had bought a new grey suit and killer heels for the occasion, wanting to look and feel my most confident. I'd also purchased a case of beer for my master, who had guided and mentored me during my articles of clerkship.

I was newly married and feeling on top of the world, like nothing could stop me. I was excited and optimistic about my legal career. I was going to make a difference in the world. I loved my work, the clients I represented and the people in my team.

That day, I took an oath of office in the Queensland Supreme Court in front of my husband, parents, friends and colleagues. I had been accepted into the legal profession and I left the courtroom with the Chief Justice's words of privilege, opportunity and integrity ringing in my ears.

INTRODUCTION

For many years, I worked hard building my legal knowledge and skills. I focussed on my clients; listening to their stories, explaining the applicable law and finding solutions to their legal problems. I filed applications in court, drafted advices, instructed experts and negotiated settlements. I loved my work but my focus slowly began to shift.

As I gained more experience, I started to focus my time and attention not on the clients but on the lawyers who were representing them. My passion for training, mentoring and inspiring other lawyers to do their very best work quickly developed. I wanted them to love their work, feel valued for their contribution and be proud of their achievements. This was the work I was meant to do.

This book is written for lawyers who feel the same way. Lawyers who want to successfully lead a team and become a leader people want to follow. This book is for the people leaders of law firms. The leaders who want to influence the next generation of lawyers and enable their firms to thrive in the future – a future where strong leadership is needed to navigate disruption, increased competition and rapid technological change. This book is about how to transform from a great technical lawyer into a great inspirational leader.

Of course, there are other types of leaders in a law firm – in particular, the *client* leaders, often referred to as "the rainmakers". These leaders play a pivotal role in the firm's growth and success. They attract new clients and win the work. They create a sustainable future for the firm. However, they often have a different mindset and skillset to the people leaders. Some client leaders may also want to lead people and grow their capability in this area, but some may want to solely focus on their client work. Both people and client leaders are needed in a law firm to ensure its success and growth.

It's been a privilege to be a part of the legal profession for more than 20 years – my entire professional career. I love lawyers. I have family members, friends and mentors who are part of the legal profession and I'm proud of the difference they make in the world. I'm passionate about lawyers loving what they do. I want them to be connected and committed to their leaders and their law firms. I want them to have the opportunity to learn and grow in their careers. I want them to soar.

My wish is that this book inspires **you** to step up into a legal leadership position, to influence and inspire your colleagues and give it your everything.

Happy reading.

Midja x

WHY DOES LEGAL LEADERSHIP MATTER NOW MORE THAN EVER?

Midja

CHAPTER 1

Why Does Legal Leadership Matter Now More Than Ever?

The legal industry is changing. There are a number of drivers responsible for this change. These include hyper-competition in the marketplace for both clients and lawyers and remarkable advances in technology. There is an unprecedented rate of uncertainty and unpredictability. Exciting and challenging times are ahead for the legal profession.

Law firms need to respond to these changes quickly. They need to think and operate differently and it starts at the top with great leadership.

RAPID TECHNOLOGICAL CHANGES

Digital disruption is changing the way law firms operate and the way law is practised. The Australian legal technology market is expanding, with 38 new tech firms being founded between 2015 and 2017.[1] Law firms are facing challenging times to adapt to Legal Tech solutions and are looking to educational institutions, such as the Centre for Legal Innovation from the College of Law, to help them navigate the unfamiliar territory.[2]

It has been estimated that 39% of jobs in the legal sector are at risk of automation.[3] Basic legal skills, such as database research and document drafting, which have traditionally been delegated to young lawyers, are already being automated by large Australian firms. But the new wave of artificial intelligence (AI) takes this one step further and involves the automation of higher-order thinking. This type of technology will find the relevant case law and legislation and apply it to the facts of a client's case.

Examples of AI in the legal industry are popping up around the world. A new product created by Adieu Legal, described as a collaborative divorce platform, combines AI with family law experts to create a "consensus accelerator", reaching property and financial settlements in a fraction of the traditional time.[4]

---

1 *Australia: State of the Legal Market*, White paper, 2018, Melbourne Law School and Thomson Reuters, p:12.

2 Ibid.

3 "Deloitte Insight: Over 100,000 legal roles to be automated," Legal IT Insider, 16th March, 2016. https://www.legaltechnology.com/latest-news/deloitte-insight-100000-legal-roles-to-be-automated/

4 "AI-based divorce platform wins Adieu Legal a thought leadership award," Australasian Legal Practice Management Association, 21st September, 2018. https://www.alpma.com.au/announcements/thought-leadership-awards-winner-announcement-2018

Online legal technology company LegalZoom is now a formidable competitor in the retail legal market in the United States. It has served approximately 3.6 million clients. These clients would have traditionally been shut out of the legal system because of access or price. Now, they can access legal services completely online with different levels of lawyer involvement based on the complexity of their problem and budget.

DoNotPay is an app that is described as a legal chatbot or robot lawyer. It "chats" with clients and takes their statement. It then uses the answers to classify the case into one of 15 different legal areas, such as breach of contract or negligence. DoNotPay draws up all the documents specific to that legal domain and fills in the details. The client prints it out, mails it to the appropriate courthouse and then they're a plaintiff. If the client must attend court in person, the bot even creates a script for them to read in the courtroom.

"I'm not saying bots will be arguing in the Supreme Court," the app's creator, Joshua Browder, said. "But for things like landlord-tenant disputes, or if you buy something and it doesn't work, or if you've been a victim of a data breach − there's no reason why that's not a clear-cut case and you will win, if you have the evidence and the damages."[5]

The challenges created by technology are, of course, not confined to the practice of law. All industries must respond and adapt to a new world. In fact, it has been suggested that the medical profession offers a glimpse into the future of law. "Physician time is now leveraged by machine, processes, other professionals and paraprofessionals. Physicians perform only high-value tasks

---

5 Bowles, J. "Who needs lawyers? DoNotPay lets you 'sue anyone' free via a chatbot," *diginomica*, 17th October, 2018. https://diginomica.com/2018/10/17/who-needs-lawyers-donotpay-lets-you-sue-anyone-free-via-a-chatbot/

that warrant their differentiated professional expertise, skills and training – machines and/or other human resources in the supply chain do the rest. Law – like medicine decades earlier – is undergoing a fundamental reshuffling of the deck."

THE COMPETITION FOR CLIENTS

There is now more competition for clients in the legal marketplace than ever before, and these clients have high expectations of their lawyers. They are savvy and demand tailored solutions to their problems. They are well-read and well-researched. This level of client sophistication is unprecedented.

And, as clients' businesses have become more complex, so too have their legal problems. Clients' issues often span jurisdictions and distinct areas of law. They are dealing with their own rapid technological changes, high volumes of data, pricing pressures and regulation challenges. Their world is changing and they need their law firm to keep up.

Clients know what they want from their lawyers. They are demanding more service for less cost. They are not afraid to replace their lawyer if their needs are not being met. The constant movement of partners between firms means clients cease using a firm when a key partner leaves. In fact, a third of companies stopped using at least one law firm in 2017 for failing to meet expectations, with 82% shifting their work to another firm and 15% bringing the work in-house until a suitable firm was identified.[6]

---

6 Walsh, K. and Tadros, E. "The big switch: why a third of companies will change lawyers," *Australian Financial Review*, 1st February, 2018. https://www.afr.com/business/legal/the-big-switch-why-a-third-of-companies-will-change-lawyers-20180129-h0q9cb

This demand from clients is not only heightening competition between existing law firms, it's also resulting in a high number of new players wanting to secure a piece of the market share. The number of law firms is set to grow at 3.6% per annum over the next five years, despite the Australian population growing at a rate of just 1.5% per annum.[7]

Competitors from other jurisdictions are making their way to the Australian market. International firms see our legal market as an opportunity to expand their practices and gain a share of revenue. These firms have the capital to invest in premises, technology and talent and are making their mark in the industry. They bring a broad spectrum of experience, skills and knowledge to the market and their multi-disciplinary services do well in solving their clients' complex problems.

Similarly, there has been an increase in acquisitions by Australian law firms of small and mid-tier operators who are benefiting from larger and more diversified offerings. In the 2018 financial year, there was a continued consolidation and expansion of large national commercial law firms, with law firm tie-ups peaking at 19 deals, involving 123 partners.[8] There was also a significant number of law firm mergers at the state-based and regional levels, with the dominant areas of expertise being corporate and commercial, property and banking and finance.[9]

In the future, law firms will not only be competing with one another. The "Big Four" accounting firms (PwC, KPMG, Deloitte and EY) are

---

7 Hugo-Hamman, R. "The 5 Big Threats Facing Small Law Firms Today," LEAP Legal Software. https://www.leap.com.au/whitepapers/5-big-threats-facing-small-law-firms-today/

8 *Australia: State of the Legal Market*, White paper, 2018, Melbourne Law School and Thomson Reuters, p:8.

9 *Australia: State of the Legal Market*, White paper, 2018, Melbourne Law School and Thomson Reuters, p:9.

developing their own legal practices as part of their one-stop shop offering.[10] This will result in an increased battle for market share and some legal work becoming highly commoditised.

On the opposite end of the spectrum is the emergence of boutique firms. These small firms are usually formed by one or two partners setting up their own practice and specialising in a specific work-type or niche client segment. These firms are having success in a market where clients value personalised service and commitment. They are not burdened with the politics, processes and bureaucracy of larger organisations and, as such, can be nimble and responsive to their clients' changing needs.

The challenge for all firms, from large internationals to boutique operations, is to meet the growing needs of clients and exceed them. The competition is red hot! Law firms need to deliver quality service and produce exceptional outcomes to keep their clients happy.

THE COMPETITION TO ATTRACT AND RETAIN TALENTED LAWYERS

In addition to the competition for clients, there is the competition for talented lawyers. Law firms are competing to become the employer of choice for top talent.

Once a law firm attracts the right lawyers, the challenge is to keep them. According to the *Australian Financial Review* Law Partnership Survey for 2018, lateral partner hires far outnumbered internal promotions (127 or 73% of new partners at the nation's leading

---

10 Murray, B. and Fortinberry, A. *Leading the Future: The Human Science of Law Firm Strategy and Leadership*. Ark Group, 2016.

firms, compared to 46).[11] This means law firms must ensure their lawyers are engaged. Lawyers, particularly partners, know their value and they know they have options in the employment market.

In the financial year 2018, a staggering 273 partners switched firms in Australia. This number doesn't even include partner movement from mergers and acquisitions. This is the highest rate of partner churn in recent years, accounting for an increase of 19% from the 2017 financial year.[12]

It's a real challenge for law firms. On the one hand, they want to keep their talented lawyers happy and engaged. But on the other hand, as competition in the market intensifies and client demands increase, law firms can be quick to want more and more from their people. They want their lawyers to work at a faster pace and produce more with less. Is this realistic? How much more can lawyers be pushed?

In most law firms, there still exists the relentless pursuit of the billable hour. Lawyers are working longer hours than ever before. The average qualified fee earner worked 13 more hours in Quarter 4 of FY 2018 than in Q4 of 2017 and 15 more hours when compared to Q4 in 2015.[13] How long can this upward trend continue? When I speak with practising lawyers, they are at their limit. There is nothing left in the tank.

So, what are current legal leaders doing to make practising law and partnership attractive to the next generation? I once read that

11 Walsh, K. and Tadros, E. "The big switch: why a third of companies will change lawyers," *Australian Financial Review*, 1st February, 2018. https://www.afr.com/business/legal/the-big-switch-why-a-third-of-companies-will-change-lawyers-20180129-h0q9cb

12 *Australia: State of the Legal Market*, White paper, 2018, Melbourne Law School and Thomson Reuters, p:10.

13 *Australia: State of the Legal Market*, White paper, 2018, Melbourne Law School and Thomson Reuters, p:6.

"making partner is like winning a pie-eating contest, only to find out the prize is more pie."[14] In other words, it takes long and difficult hours to make partner for even longer and more difficult hours.

This stressful work environment is pushing members of the legal profession to their physical and emotional limits. Surveys suggest that in the case of solicitors, one in three at any one stage are suffering depression, high anxiety and stress.[15] Something has to change.

CHANGING BUSINESS MODELS AND LAW FIRM STRUCTURES

The final area of change is the way law firms are structuring their businesses. The traditional equity partnership model is being replaced by incorporated entities. Some of these are listing on the stock exchange. This allows them to raise the funds to better compete in the marketplace and with the Big Four in particular. It also means the traditional role of partner will look very different in the future, and partners will most likely become employees and possibly shareholders rather than equity owners of the business. Traditional tenure at one or two law firms in a lawyer's career may become a thing of the past as more and more lawyers become self-employed individuals working for one or more businesses.

The challenge for these law firms is how to maximise the success of the corporate governance model. They must fulfil their duty to the court first and foremost, but they must also fulfil their duties

---

14 Peckman, M. "How Making Partner Is Like Winning a Pie-Eating Contest," Law.com, 1st February, 2008. https://www.law.com/almID/900005502254/?slreturn=20181019135036

15 Marcus, C. "Lawyers' alarming depression rates prompt efforts to boost mental health support," ABC News, 21st November, 2014. https://www.abc.net.au/news/2014-11-21/lawyers-depression-rates-alarming/5903660

to shareholders. Along with these duties is the requirement of accurate market reporting and forecasting.

There is also the question of what leadership looks like when leaders are fixed-term CEOs and executive members as opposed to lifelong equity partners. In the 2018 financial year, senior leadership and C-Suite appointments focussed on innovation and expertise from adjacent professional services industries, in particular a connection to and background in the Big Four firms.[16] We may see this trend continue into the future with the increase in market competition and complexity of clients' problems.

SO, WHAT CAN BE DONE?

If law firms are to survive and thrive in this fluctuating and competitive future market, they need to develop great leaders. Law firms can no longer simply pluck their best technical lawyers and appoint them as people managers, hoping they will rise to the occasion. They need to take a more strategic approach.

> *"There are too many specialists, too many black-letter lawyers, and too many legal technicians. Few of these will be needed in the firms of the future. What will be needed will be men and women who understand the art of listening, questioning and giving advice in a way that gives clients a sense of safety."[17]*

Law firms need to invest in the leadership development of their lawyers from the beginning of their careers. They must build their lawyers' legal expertise and leadership skills concurrently. Law

---

16 *Australia: State of the Legal Market*, White paper, 2018, Melbourne Law School and Thomson Reuters, p:11.

17 Murray, B. and Fortinberry, *A. Leading the Future: The Human Science of Law Firm Strategy and Leadership*. Ark Group, 2016.

firms do not have enough ready-now leaders. One HR professional told me she could pinpoint the time when her firm pulled back on its professional development and leadership training. The firm is now scrambling to backfill its leadership positions.

Some lawyers are rising to the challenge of leadership and flourishing, but many more are floundering. They don't have the skills, confidence or knowledge to lead. It's time for this to change. The challenge for law firms is to make leadership development a top priority. Often, the first consideration is the cost involved. What if we train them and they go? Well, what if you don't train them and they stay? Lawyers expect their firm to play a pivotal role in their personal and professional development. They expect a partnership where they give their best to the firm and the firm provides them with growth and learning opportunities in return.

Research by KBE Human Capital shows that market-leading law firms are investing time and energy into leadership development, implementing sustainable work practices and facilitating holistic/soft-skills training. In other words, they are valuing their people and their development. According to KBE, "These leadership teams also work hard to ensure their business strategy/KPIs are geared towards building long-term win/win client relationships ahead of short-term profits."[18]

Effective leadership is needed to attract the very best lawyers – in particular, lawyers who are aligned with a firm's culture and values. Lawyers need inspirational leadership, they need to believe in something, they need to connect and feel a sense of belonging. The legal industry needs more leaders that people want to follow. If law firms fail to invest in the leadership development of their lawyers,

18 Ryan, E. "'Decisive' leadership the winning ingredient for law firm success," *LawyersWeekly*, 13th September, 2018. https://www.lawyersweekly.com.au/mobile-menu-item-5/24028-decisive-leadership-the-winning-ingredient-for-law-firm-success

they will be left behind. They will lose their successful lawyers, their most productive assets, to other firms and organisations. The lawyers who stay will lack engagement and commitment and experience high levels of stress and burnout. These law firms will lack the collaboration and innovation needed to compete in the market.

The future leaders of law firms must drive positive change and innovation. They must make the most of the opportunities changing technology presents them with and leverage Legal Tech solutions to serve their clients and allow their lawyers to work smarter, not harder. AI technology will allow lawyers to focus on higher-value work for their clients and enable law firms to work more efficiently and with greater flexibility. It will bring a wonderful opportunity for law firms to change their focus from transactional process skills to "human" skills.

Our leaders and our lawyers need to embrace a new way of working. According to Richard Susskind, law futurist and author of the book *The End of Lawyers?*, we need a new kind of lawyer who is trained in the skills AI is not capable of automating. These include creativity, empathy, compassion and human intelligence. The lawyers who can develop these skills will flourish in the new AI landscape and become the top legal leaders.

The core legal work performed by lawyers will continue to narrow. Clients require integrated solutions to their complex problems. To compete with the Big Four, law firms will need to think and operate differently and develop "multiple business competencies", which means offering traditional legal advice along with data management, analytics, technical support and strategic planning.[19]

19 Cohen, M. "The Legal Industry Needs Fresh Leadership with New Skill Sets," *Forbes*, 18th September, 2017. https://www.forbes.com/sites/markcohen1/2017/09/18/the-legal-industry-needs-fresh-leadership-with-new-skill-sets/#6761dbf267d7

CHAPTER 1

There is no turning back and no room for complacency. Law firms and their lawyers need to be prepared for the future. We need a different leadership culture, one that is agile, innovative, strategic, collaborative and transparent.

It's time for change.

WHY TRANSFORM FROM GREAT LAWYER TO GREAT LEADER?

CHAPTER 2

Why Transform From Great Lawyer to Great Leader?

What's In It For You?

The legal profession needs great leaders who thrive in times of uncertainty, change and disruption. Law firms are changing their structures, the way they do business, how they leverage technology and the way they provide high-quality service to their clients. They need legal leaders who can inspire and gain greater commitment from their people to deliver innovative solutions. They need leaders who are confident and highly collaborative.

This is a time of unique opportunity for you. You're an experienced lawyer who has dedicated your time and focus on your specific area of legal expertise to meet your clients' demands. Are you ready to step away from doing the client work yourself to focus on coaching and developing the people in your firm? Are you ready to take the lead?

There could be some hesitation. Perhaps you fear stepping up into a leadership role. You may fear the unknown, having to start again with a new set of skills. You may be thinking, "I'm at the top of my game. I'm a great lawyer. I know what I'm doing and I don't particularly want to learn a new set of skills and a new approach to work."

No doubt you have a strong reputation as a great lawyer. Maybe it's easier to stick to what you know – your clients, the law and running cases. You could be questioning, "What if I step up into a leadership position and fail? My people will become disengaged. They won't want to be a part of my team and I won't achieve my goals. What if I have to ask for help? Am I willing to do this?"

Let's face it, leading lawyers is a tough gig. It's a role that involves understanding the Millennial generation in the workplace – what they want and how to motivate them. On the other end of the spectrum, it involves leading lawyers who have more experience than you, who have been admitted for longer and who might be the highly valued rainmakers of the firm.

I understand all of this may be enough to turn you off a leadership position. In fact, it's been said that managing lawyers is like herding cats – nearly impossible![1]

Indeed, there are a lot of moving parts when it comes to leading people. There's uncertainty and unpredictability. Feelings and

---

[1] Richard, L. "Herding Cats: The Lawyer Personality Revealed," LawyerBrain. http://www.lawyerbrain.com/sites/default/files/caliper_herding_cats.pdf

emotions make their impact. There is a high degree of vulnerability when stepping into such a role. You must share more of who you are and what you believe in. You must let people in and this can seem daunting.

All these fears and concerns are, of course, understandable and normal.

However, the good news is that if you take the leap, if you believe in yourself and take up the challenge of leadership, it will reward you tenfold. It will put you in a position to make a significant difference in your law firm and the legal industry. You will gain a deeper understanding of who you are and what you're capable of. It will expand your thinking and develop your skillset. It will step you out of your comfort zone and grow your self-confidence.

You *can* become a leader with following. You can gain trust and commitment from your team. You can influence and bring about positive change. You can create a vision for your people and deliver exceptional service and results to your clients.

If you've picked up this book, I bet that there's a big part of you that wants to lead. A part of you that wants to inspire, create a connection with your people and, ultimately, make a difference in their lives.

So, let's talk about how we can make that happen.

HOW TO BECOME A GREAT LEGAL LEADER

CHAPTER 3

How to Become a Great Legal Leader

A Leader Worth Following

As a highly successful lawyer, you've been praised for your legal expertise, your productivity and your billings. Now, you've made the decision to step into a leadership role. Guess what? The game has changed. The goal posts have been moved and what got you here is not going to get you there.

In her book, *Lawyers as Leaders*, author and researcher Deborah Rhode states: "My central claim is that the legal profession attracts a number of individuals with the ambition and the analytic capabilities to be leaders, but frequently fails to develop other qualities that are essential to effectiveness."[1]

---

1 Rhodes, D. *Lawyers as Leaders*, Oxford University Press, 2013.

CHAPTER 3

If you want your ambition of leadership to come to fruition, it's time to develop these other qualities.

Research conducted by Dr Larry Richard at the Hildebrandt Institute indicates that, on average, lawyers score significantly higher than the rest of the population in six key behavioural traits.[2] They are:

1. Highly sceptical
2. High sense of urgency
3. Autonomous
4. Low sociability
5. Low resilience
6. Resistant to new ideas

When I look at these traits, they certainly feel familiar to me as a lawyer. Are any of them familiar to you? It's important you consider whether you exhibit any of these traits and what impact they may have on your success as a leader.

As a lawyer, you have acquired the mindset, behaviours and skills to perform at your legal best. These qualities have served you well but now it's time to consider what you need to change to step into a leadership position. Some of the qualities and skills essential to being a great lawyer can be challenges when you want to transform into a great leader. A good dose of self-awareness is what's needed.

So, what does it take to successfully make this transformation? You must fulfil three critical areas of leadership development:

2 Leeke, S. "The Importance of Developing Leadership in Law Firms," Thomson Reuters, 24th July, 2014. http://insight.thomsonreuters.com.au/posts/importance-developing-leadership-in-law-firms

1. MINDSET

The first step is to develop a leadership mindset. You need to think differently as a leader than you do as a lawyer. It's about shifting the way you see your world, your work and the value you offer. It all starts with you and what's going on inside your head. This internal shift in thinking must happen first. You must lead yourself before you can lead others.

2. IDENTITY

The next step is to gain clarity on your identity as a leader. You have spent a long time as a lawyer and it's likely your self-worth and self-value are somewhat dependent on this role. For many years, the focus has been on billings and client development. You now need to see your value differently. You know who you are as a lawyer, now it's time to find out who you are as a leader. Ask yourself, "Who am I now and how do I add value to the world?"

It's time to recalibrate. Get up close and personal with yourself. Hold up the mirror and take a good look at what you see, then consider what you would like to see.

3. SKILLSET

Now, it's time to put 1 and 2 into action and connect and lead your people. It's time to stop focussing on yourself and start focussing on them. This means building an emotional connection. By appealing to your people's purpose, you can inspire greatness.

It's time to put on a different tool belt. Yes, you need to keep some tools used in your role as a lawyer, but it's time to add some new leadership tools to your belt.

THE GREAT LAWYER TO GREAT LEADER MODEL

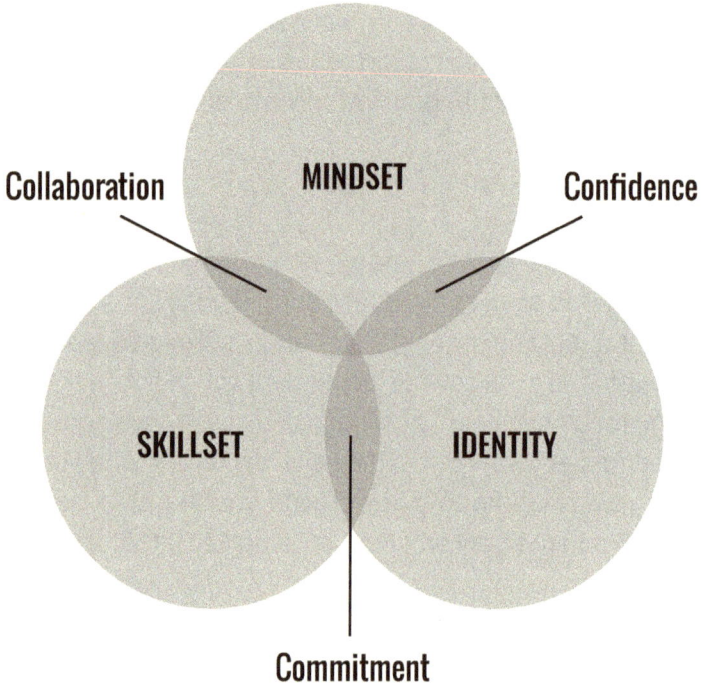

CONFIDENCE: You gain the confidence to lead your people

At the intersection of **Mindset** and **Identity** is CONFIDENCE. This is when you have made the choice to lead and have shifted your mindset from lawyer to leader.

In my first book, *Confidence – How to be Your Most Authentic, Courageous and Unshakeable Self,* I discuss what it takes to become an unshakeable leader – a leader who is strong, determined and impactful.

When you're unshakeable, you have a deep understanding of who you are as a leader and how you add the most value to your organisation. You lead with authenticity and congruence. You're comfortable in your own skin.

You've let go of being right and instead, you've become curious about the opinions of others. Your focus has changed and you can give your opinions freely without fear of judgement or rejection. You can accept criticism and feedback.

You have the confidence to set higher goals for yourself and your team, and you're ready and willing to accept greater responsibilities. You have a determined and tenacious resolution to achieve your goals and make the difference you were meant to make. You stretch yourself and others.

You have the courage to take risks and step outside your comfort zone, knowing this is the space of personal growth and development. By doing so, you encourage others to do the same. Confidence is easy to catch and when you're unshakeable, you pass it on.

Without confidence, you can suffer from the imposter syndrome. This is the persistent fear of being exposed as a fraud in your leadership position. It's that voice in your head that says, "What are you doing here? They're going to find you out!" Sound familiar? It does to me and I'm not alone. Researchers believe that up to 70% of people have suffered from imposter syndrome at some point.[3] It's a common experience.

---

3 Warrell, M. "Afraid Of Being 'Found Out'? How To Overcome Imposter Syndrome," *Forbes*, 3rd April, 2014. https://www.forbes.com/sites/margiewarrell/2014/04/03/impostor-syndrome/#10d928a748a9

CHAPTER 3

Imposter syndrome may take the form of perfectionism; the belief you need to be perfect at everything to be successful in your role. You discount praise from others and believe your goals have been achieved through sheer luck rather than your own efforts. You worry about not being "enough". The fear of failure – the fear you will be unable to deliver and disappoint everyone – can be overwhelming.

These feelings lead to low self-confidence and increased self-doubt. You dwell on your mistakes and failures. Imposter syndrome keeps you in your comfort zone, under the radar. You don't want to be seen in case you are judged negatively by others. You stay safe and may even sabotage yourself because you don't feel you deserve success. You may even make the decision that leadership is not for you and step away from a position of influence.

Despite this, I believe this worry and stress comes from a good place. It means you want to achieve great things. The key is to acknowledge and embrace these feelings and use them to move forward in your leadership career. Use them to achieve your best, not stop you in your tracks or send you backwards. Confidence is the key.

I am not afraid.
I was born to do this.

JOAN OF ARC

COMMITMENT: You gain the commitment from your people

At the intersection of **Identity** and **Skillset** is COMMITMENT. There is harmony between what you stand for as a leader, what you do and how you treat your people. Once your people experience this authenticity from you, they will commit to you and your team's shared vision and goals.

If you want to have influence as a leader, commitment instead of compliance is needed from every team member. Let's discuss the difference between the two.

WHAT IS COMPLIANCE?

IT LOOKS LIKE:	IT SOUNDS LIKE:	IT FEELS LIKE:
An empty office at 5.01pm every day. People slumped over their desks, wearing their "screen-saver faces". People just going through the motions.	"Sorry, that's not my job," "Friday? That's just not possible." It sounds like a lot of no, no, no!	Hard work. It's demotivating and disheartening.

What's the Result of Compliance?

If you only have compliance from your team members, you have low trust. As a leader, you will merely have positional power with little real influence. Your people will say and do all the right things in front of you but will show disrespect and disobedience behind your back. This will result in you having to micromanage their performance, only to achieve acceptable results at best. People will only do the minimal level of work required and nothing more. There will be low engagement and low alignment, resulting in a stagnant workplace with little growth or innovation. Doesn't sound like a great place to work, does it?

Now, let's compare that to commitment.

WHAT IS COMMITMENT?

IT LOOKS LIKE:	IT SOUNDS LIKE:	IT FEELS LIKE:
Commitment looks like purposeful and focussed work. People are smiling, making eye contact and walking with their shoulders back.	It sounds like, "What else is possible?", "How can I help?", "How do we make that happen by Friday?" It sounds like yes, yes, yes!	It feels like belonging to a tribe – purposeful, in flow. Work is no longer work.

What's the Result of Commitment?

When you gain genuine commitment from your people, there is a high level of trust and loyalty in your team. You gain influence and engagement as a leader with low turnover and absenteeism. There is personal accountability and self-leadership, which means you can stop micro-managing and start being creative and innovative. Your team achieves great results and goes above and beyond to get the job done, exceeding your expectations. There's excitement, anticipation and agility in the workplace.

As a great legal leader, you need to strive for commitment from each team member. Watch the signals and ask yourself, "What do I see? What do I hear? What do I feel?" Answer truthfully whether you have compliance or commitment and ask yourself what you can do to gain more commitment from your team members.

There's always a way
— if you are committed.

TONY ROBBINS

COLLABORATION: You embrace collaboration as a way of working together

At the intersection of **Skillset** and **Mindset** is COLLABORATION. This is where lawyers work together to solve client problems. Collaboration brings about a sustainable competitive advantage in the marketplace. Until the law firm's performance is more important than an individual lawyer's, it will remain difficult to implement firm-focussed strategies.[4]

Collaboration creates a culture of innovation and creative solutions. As we've already discussed, clients' legal issues are becoming more complex. These issues often need knowledge and expertise outside your own niche. It is only with the help of other lawyers that you can provide a full solution to the client. Each lawyer must

---

4 Letterman White, S. "Leadership: Do We Have It All Wrong?" *Law Practice Today*, 12th October, 2017. https://www.lawpracticetoday.org/article/leadership-do-we-have-it-wrong/

play to their strengths, bringing their own expertise and experience to the table. Different lawyers will produce different solutions and their ideas can be built upon to create something truly unique.

Together we are better. Of course, this means the law firm must have processes in place that not only support this way of working but reward it.

Collaboration also leads to formal and informal learning opportunities. It creates a learning environment where people are informally mentored by others who have different skills and expertise. People get exposed to different ways of thinking. Everyone gets to share their experiences and points of view. They feel truly valued, which nurtures their confidence and self-belief.

Collaboration builds connections between your people, strengthening their working relationships. They feel like they are part of a team, which means a higher retention rate for your firm. It's much harder to leave this type of experience.

So, if collaboration has so many benefits, why can it be difficult to foster in a law firm? The two greatest barriers to collaboration are:

1. **A lack of confidence in yourself.** If you don't have a healthy dose of self-confidence (as discussed earlier), you can't allow yourself to be open to other people's opinions. You will fail to truly listen to them. You'll want to stick to your own opinions and prove how right you are. Collaboration takes confidence and humility.

2. **A lack of trust in others.** A great leader needs the right mindset and leadership capabilities, which we will discuss in the coming chapters, to build enough trust to allow

collaboration to happen. In the words of Stephen Covey, "Without trust we don't truly collaborate; we merely coordinate or, at best, cooperate. It is trust that transforms a group of people into a team."

It is this combination of confidence, commitment and collaboration that will transform you from great lawyer to great leader.

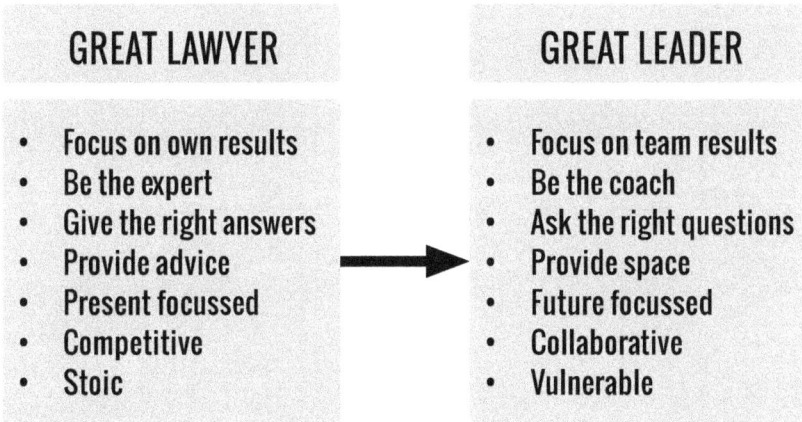

GREAT LAWYER	GREAT LEADER
• Focus on own results	• Focus on team results
• Be the expert	• Be the coach
• Give the right answers	• Ask the right questions
• Provide advice	• Provide space
• Present focussed	• Future focussed
• Competitive	• Collaborative
• Stoic	• Vulnerable

CHAPTER 4

LEADERSHIP MINDSET

CHAPTER 4.1

Get Curious

Accept Uncertainty

Many years ago, I was lucky enough to spend some time with corporate anthropologist Michael Henderson. Our firm had engaged Michael to study its culture.

Michael and I visited our offices, interviewed staff, asked questions and observed. Michael spent a lot of time watching and listening. Someone would make a comment in a meeting or Michael would see something in the office and he would pull out his little moleskin notebook and write down his observations. He had an inquisitive nature – I suppose it comes with being an anthropologist. The biggest lesson I took away from my work with Michael was the power of curiosity.

Curiosity is a fundamental ingredient of great leadership. As a leader, you need to have a hungry mind and a willingness to learn. This is more important now than ever because we are working in a fast-paced, innovative and uncertain business environment.

CHAPTER 4.1

When asked recently to name the number-one attribute CEOs will need to succeed in the turbulent times ahead, Michael Dell, chief executive of Dell Technologies, replied: "I would place my bet on curiosity." Dell was responding to a 2015 PwC survey of more than 1,000 CEOs, many of whom cited curiosity and open-mindedness as the traits that are becoming increasingly critical to great leadership in challenging times.[1]

Curiosity as a leader results in two things:

1. You will be less judgmental and more accepting of diverse opinions. You will seek first to understand. Your people will feel valued and they'll feel listened to.

2. You will be able to accept ambiguity and uncertainty. You will be energised by the complexity of a leadership situation rather than intimidated by it. You will be able to handle being uncomfortable, you will experiment and you'll take risks.

It's a bit like doing a huge jigsaw puzzle. At the start, there are pieces everywhere. It's all over the place. You have a few bits over here that go together and a few bits over there that look similar. You might get all the corner pieces in place. The most important thing is to stay with the uncertainty. Don't get discouraged by the fact that you don't know how everything will fit together. Over time, by staying with your curiosity and the uncertainty, the puzzle starts coming together. You say, "Oh, I see now. These pieces belong over here. And that blue section is actually the sea, not the sky. Oh, I've got it." There is a new and deeper level of understanding. The process gets faster and you end up finishing the puzzle and achieving the result.

1 Berger, W. "Why Curious People Are Destined for the C-Suite," *Harvard Business Review*, 11th September, 2015. https://hbr.org/2015/09/why-curious-people-are-destined-for-the-c-suite

Leading with curiosity is like that. Sometimes, one piece of the puzzle or situation doesn't make sense in isolation. You need to find out more. You have to ask more questions. You must discover the context of the situation, learn more and be OK with the uncertainty. Once you gain a greater understanding, you can move into action and start making effective, well-informed decisions.

If you lack curiosity as a leader, you'll become stagnant and conservative. You won't take risks or push boundaries. You'll rush decisions in your need for certainty and closure instead of seeking new ideas. You'll end up doing everything you can to validate your own opinion in your need to be "right". This will result in little creativity or innovation in your team and law firm.

Your role as a leader is to be inquisitive and future focussed and to inspire people to follow you down a new path.

IDEAS TO BECOME MORE CURIOUS:

- Seek new influences, ideas and experiences. Not just from the legal profession, but from other industries.

- Spend more time asking questions. We'll talk more about this in the coming chapters.

- Admit your mistakes and learn from them.

- Generate ideas from your team members and ask for their opinions.

- Question your assumptions and beliefs.

- Let go of having to be right. See Chapter 4.2 on this.

- Commit to being a lifelong learner.

- Routinely ask yourself reflection questions, such as: How can I continue to grow as a leader? What do I fear right now? What challenges do I face? What can I do to create more meaningful relationships?

We keep moving forward, opening up new doors and doing new things because we're curious and curiosity keeps leading us down new paths.

WALT DISNEY

CHAPTER 4.2

Let Go of Being Right

Value Differences

"The way the law is largely practised invites lawyers to solve problems by first making them bigger and by then aggressively holding a position until a decision is imposed or a compromise based on brinkmanship is reached."
– Ann-Marie Rice[1]

To influence others and gain commitment, leaders need to take a very different approach to problem-solving. They need to let go of the need to be right.

Being right feels good, doesn't it? It makes you feel confident, worthy and valuable. As a lawyer, you get paid to provide the

---

1 Rice, A. "Law is 'inherently masculine' but women can help change it," *LawyersWeekly*, 31st October, 2018. https://www.lawyersweekly.com.au/biglaw/24349-law-is-inherently-masculine-but-women-can-help-change-it

right solution for your clients. You have your own strong ideas and opinions based on your years of experience and vast legal knowledge. You want to share this knowledge and you genuinely believe your approach to problem-solving is right. But, of course, it's only *your* way, not *the* way. This can be difficult to accept.

If you think you're right about everything and always go with your own ideas, your people stop thinking for themselves. Why would they bother to think creatively and share their point of view when it's never listened to or considered? They'll quickly learn their opinions are not valued.

It is important, as a leader, that you allow your viewpoint to be challenged. You also need to be open to changing your own mind about a situation. This can be perceived as a weakness in a leader; however, it actually demonstrates the opposite. When you're secure and confident enough, you can admit when you're wrong.

> *Faced with the choice between changing one's mind and proving that there is no need to do so, almost everyone gets busy on the proof.*
>
> JOHN GALBRAITH

Effective leaders don't feel threatened when their opinions are challenged. They are the first ones to say, "I hadn't thought about it that way. Let's give it a try." And when you let go of being right, you can genuinely value the diversity in your team. You value feedback.

I remember once I was engaged in a conversation with the in-house counsel at a law firm. I was discussing the idea of doing after-case reviews with the in-house counsel, the solicitors involved and the paralegals or any other staff who had worked on the case. I discussed the concept of conducting an informal meeting around what worked well and what we would do differently next time. I said, "So, the great thing about this is it will give us an opportunity to learn from one another – for the lawyers and paralegals to learn, and for yourself as in-house counsel to learn as well."

The in-house counsel looked at me and said, "What do you mean? There'd be nothing I could learn from one of the junior lawyers." I looked at him expecting him to laugh like it was a joke. But he didn't. He was dead serious that, as in-house counsel and a senior practitioner, he would have nothing to learn from the solicitor who briefed him.

What a missed opportunity! No matter how senior we are, no matter what's written on our business card, we can always learn from others. That's one of the traits of a great leader. They're always open to learning from others and they value the differences others bring to the discussion.

Now, I must admit that when I started in a leadership position, I struggled to genuinely value the differences of the people in my team.

I was naturally drawn to people who thought and acted like me. Those were the people I wanted to work with. They behaved the way I did and they agreed with me on everything.

Then there were other people in the team who were different to me. They slowed me down, they challenged my ideas and they behaved in a very different way to me. To be honest, for a long time, these people annoyed me! I tolerated them but did I value them? Absolutely not. If I had my way, I would have taken them off my team and replaced them with people like me.

Now when I admit that, it makes me shudder. What was I thinking? A bunch of mini Midjas? What a disaster!

As leaders, we need to have people around us who are different to us — people who behave differently, see things differently and complement our skill set. Of course, you want to have a shared vision and a strong set of aligned values and beliefs, but when it comes to how you work, you want the people in your team to be different. It will be those differences that make your team truly special.

It's the acceptance of other people's viewpoints and letting go of being right which also allows you to ask for help. Sometimes as a lawyer, you might be reluctant to ask for help. You'll recall from Chapter 2 that lawyers rate highly in the trait of autonomy. Lawyers want to be independent.

If you're like me, you have this image of yourself as a strong, independent and capable lawyer. But just because you're all those things doesn't mean you don't need others or that you should feel any less for putting your hand up and admitting you need help.

It's a little like having a flare gun as a safety precaution in your boat. The flare gun is there for a reason. You shouldn't wait until the boat is sinking and your head is just above the water to discharge the flare. By then it's too late, you're going under. You need to recognise when you need help. Have the courage to use your flare, ask for assistance and reach out to a trusted friend or colleague.

Does it feel scary to ask for help? Yes. Does it feel vulnerable? You bet. But if you continue to struggle with an issue, to worry about something and keep it inside you, it will get bigger. It will consume you.

There was a time recently when I was worried. The kind of worry that keeps you up at night and wakes you in the early hours of the morning. Finally, after a week of worrying, I decided to pick up the phone and ask a friend for help. It took a couple of text messages and a good dose of courage but I did it.

There will be lots of moments when you're not sure what you're doing in your leadership role, when it feels like you're stumbling in the dark. The secret is to know when to send up the flare and who to.

The fear of being vulnerable and being labelled "soft" or "weak" as a leader can hold you back. You worry people will think less of you, that you're not coping in your role. You think it will negatively impact your reputation and brand. However, US researcher and writer Brené Brown says the number-one trust-earning behaviour at work is asking for help. So, it's time to let go of the negative beliefs we have about reaching out to others and admitting we need their support. As Brown says, "Until we can receive with an open heart, we're never really giving with an open heart. When we attach judgment to receiving help, we knowingly or unknowingly attach judgment to giving help."[2]

As a leader, letting go of being right and asking for help will build your reputation as a strong yet humble leader. It will create robust relationships with your people and make them feel valued.

---

2 Brown, B. *The Gifts of Imperfection: Let Go of Who You Think You're Supposed to Be and Embrace Who You Are*, Hazelden Publishing, 2010.

CHAPTER 4.2

When you ask for help, it:

- Humanises you as a leader. You're real and authentic. How refreshing.

- Allows others to feel safe to ask for help, too. You set the unwritten ground rules as the leader. If you can do it, so can everyone else.

- Creates a collaborative rather than competitive culture. It leaves ego at the door. No one knows everything (not even the boss) and we all need help sometimes.

- Allows you to learn and grow from others. You get to ask more questions, receive advice and see your problem from a different perspective.

- Most importantly, it builds high-trust relationships.

Get Comfortable with Being Uncomfortable

Stay Green and Growing

As leaders, we are one of two things. We're either green and growing or ripe and rotting. Which would you rather be?

When I think about this, my mind immediately visualises a beautiful flowering tree. This tree has a strong trunk and root system with delicate buds – new growth, new opportunities – that, over time, open to reveal beautiful flowers.

When I think of myself as a leader, I want to be that flowering tree. I want to grow and expand. I want to accept change, feel excited about it and embrace opportunities.

CHAPTER 4.3

So, how can you stay green and growing as you lead your team? You must keep the concepts of abundance, growth and potential front of mind.

You must always take action. Do something to move forward, even if it's just a small step. Just as in nature, if you want to survive your environment, you must find a way to grow despite the conditions. Think of a concrete footpath with a tiny crack in one section. A plant emerges from this crack, determined and strong. If you ever feel like there's no way through, find that tiny crack, that one thing you can do to keep growing.

If you want to be a great leader, you must commit to being a lifelong learner. You must find ways to expand your knowledge and your thinking, to always ask yourself what is possible. You must continually work your way through the Four Stages of Learning or, as it's often referred to, the Conscious Competence Ladder. This model was developed by Noel Burch, an employee with Gordon Training International, in the 1970s. It highlights two factors that affect our thinking as we learn a new skill: consciousness (awareness) and skill level (competence).

According to the Conscious Competence Ladder, you move through the following levels as you build competence in a new skill:

Unconsciously competent	You don't know that you have this skill (it just seems easy).
Consciously competent	You know that you have this skill.
Consciously incompetent	You know that you don't have this skill.
Unconsciously incompetent	You don't know that you don't have this skill or that you need to learn it.

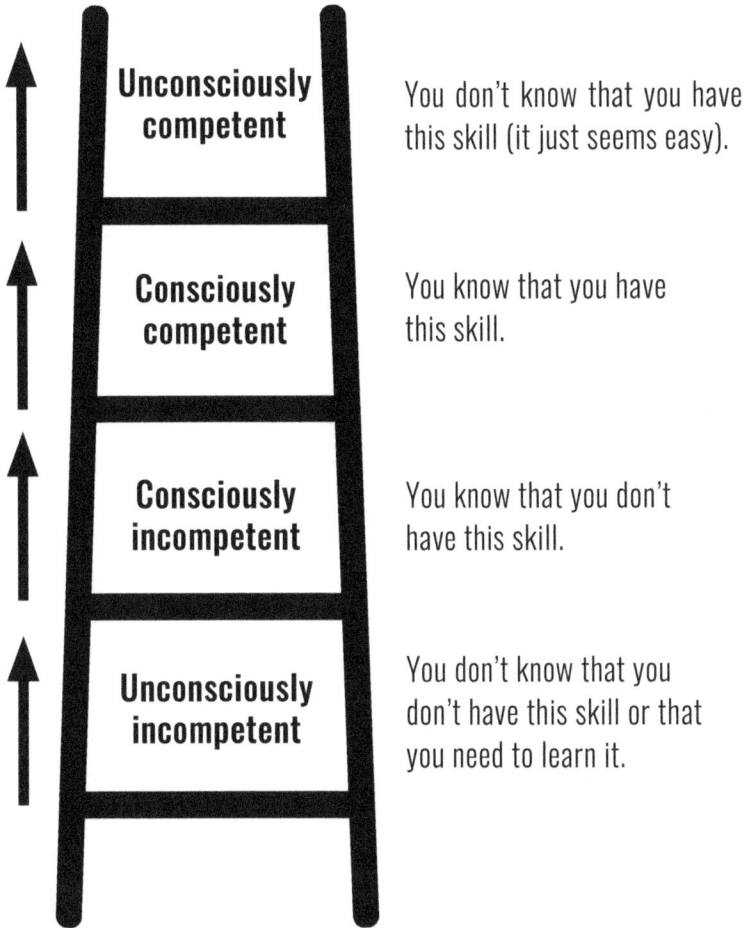

As we've discussed, up until now, you've probably spent your career honing your skills and gaining the knowledge you need to become an expert lawyer. I spent 20 years in the corporate world both as a lawyer and as an in-house facilitator and coach. I was at the highest level on the ladder, unconsciously competent. I got to the stage where I didn't even have to think about what I was doing, it just came naturally. I could get up in the morning, facilitate a course, run an induction program, coach a colleague and not have to consciously think about it.

It feels good to be in this position. You feel confident and in control. You might feel that way in your role as a lawyer right now. So, what's the downside? The problem is that you know your stuff so well, you're working inside your comfort zone.

Your comfort zone is a beautiful place. It's where you feel secure and protected. But if you want to play the leadership game, there are times when you need to step out and take a risk. You must get comfortable with being uncomfortable.

There is a part of each of us that loves routine and pattern. In your comfort zone, there is little stress and little risk. But there is also little opportunity for you to get to know yourself and what you can achieve. New experiences bring out different responses. Sometimes, you need to challenge yourself and see what is revealed.

Neuroscience tells us we need to get out of our comfort zone to rewire our brain. It is possible to train your brain to respond to challenges in new, more effective ways. But to do so, you need to experience new things.

A good friend of mine always asks, "What else is possible?" I love this question. Until you try, you don't know. So, try something new. You may surprise yourself.

I read once that the role of leaders is climate control – to create a climate of possibilities. In this climate, you and your team members will develop new skills and capabilities to face even greater challenges. Leadership is not about standing still and accepting the status quo. It's about improvement, innovation, exploration and, at times, pushing the boundaries.

Stepping outside your comfort zone can feel awkward and uncomfortable. But outside your comfort zone is a place of great opportunity. Outside your comfort zone, you are green and growing!

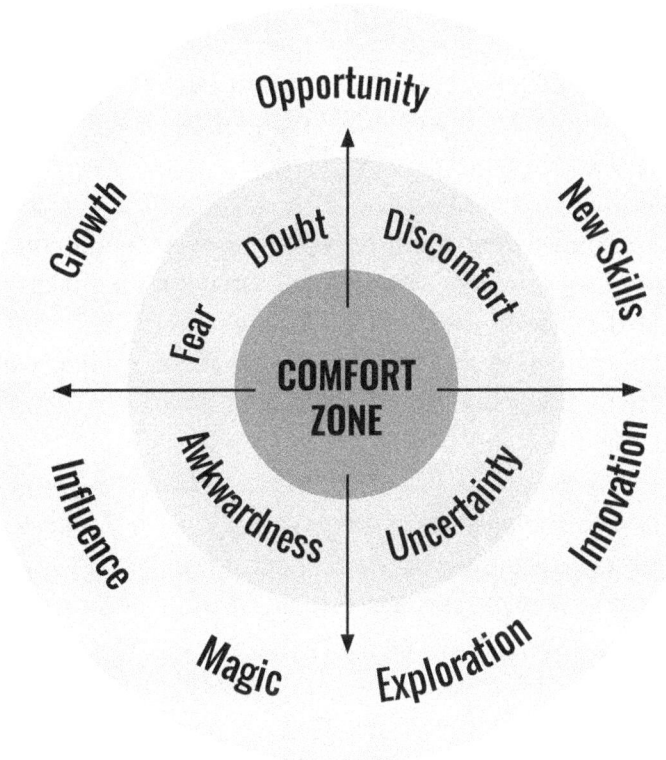

When you take the bold leap out of your comfort zone and into a new leadership position, you step back down the Conscious Competence Ladder to unconsciously incompetent. You don't know what you don't know. The result of this is actually very positive (at least, for a while). You feel optimistic, excited and ready to take on the challenge. No fear. You think to yourself, "I can do this!" Your motivation, engagement and confidence levels are high.

CHAPTER 4.3

But what happens? At some point, the bubble bursts. It bursts sooner for some people than others.

You start to learn and gain some experience. You make mistakes. Things take you a long time to do. You might start getting negative feedback from your boss, colleagues and clients. You engage a mentor who asks you some tough questions you don't know the answers to. You look around and notice that others are ahead of you in this new game of leadership. They know more than you and they have a lot more proficiency.

I experienced this when I first set up my own leadership practice. I was ready to go, unconsciously incompetent. All smiles. Then I realised there was a whole lot more to this game than I was aware of. Marketing, positioning, sales, social media, website development, invoicing, book publication, finance ... absolutely overwhelming!

This becomes the pivotal moment, your moment of choice. You feel extremely vulnerable. You feel uncomfortable and out of your depth. Sometimes, you feel plain stupid. You hate feeling this way. What makes it worse is that you've previously been at the top of your game. You've been the gun lawyer. You've been highly successful, recognised and rewarded. This change can knock your confidence and be downright scary.

If you want to keep moving forward, now is the time for you to push through the stage of consciously incompetent. It takes courage to do this. Sometimes, it feels a whole lot easier to go back to what you know and what you are good at. It can be so tempting.

If you keep doing the hard work, one day you will reach the top of the ladder again and become unconsciously competent in your new role. It's going to feel clunky at times and it's going to take a lot of commitment but it's worth it. You'll regain that feeling of control and confidence and you'll be willing to learn more and step even further outside your comfort zone. Always green and growing!

IDEAS FOR STEPPING OUT OF YOUR COMFORT ZONE:

- Acknowledge your feelings. Know that your feelings are normal and be comfortable with being uncomfortable.

- Be open to learning from different sources. Don't be afraid to ask for help. This is a new game for you.

- Find yourself a mentor to clarify your next steps, work through any barriers and keep yourself accountable.

- Follow your passion and remember the reason why you are doing what you are doing. Connect with your purpose.

- Reframe your thinking about new situations and experiences. Instead of feeling nervous, feel excited.

- Do the hard work. Hard work is what will move you forward to becoming consciously competent. My mentor often says to me, "Midja, you're just on the wrong side of a whole lot of hard work!"

CHAPTER 4.4

Create Positive Thoughts

Be a Tigger

Positivity is an often-overlooked quality of a great leader. Jack Welch, former CEO of General Electric, describes positivity as "the capacity to go-go-go with healthy vigour and an upbeat attitude through good times and bad."[1]

Positive energy is infectious. It can make such a difference to the attitude of your people. I think we've all had a leader we were cautious around every morning until we found out what mood they were in that day. It's not a great way to work.

Every day, you have the choice to choose your attitude. There is such power in this. In his book, *The Last Lecture*, Randy Pausch

---

1 Welch, J. "Are Leaders Born or Made? Here's What's Coachable — and What's Definitely Not," LinkedIn, 2nd May, 2016.

references the characters from Winnie The Pooh and says we all have a choice to make: you can be a fun-loving Tigger or a gloomy Eeyore. I know which one I would rather be and work with. Leadership involves seeing the glass half full. It's about being mindful of what's going on inside your head.

The most important words you will ever say are the words you say to yourself. It's that little voice in your head, your inner dialogue, that significantly impacts your mood and your self-belief.

So, what stories do you tell yourself? What's the script running through your head? How do you truly feel when you look in the mirror? What limits have you put in place? You can talk yourself into or out of anything. When you put negative thoughts into your conscious mind, you act a certain way. What you think impacts your behaviour and it's easy to only see the negative side of yourself and every situation.

It's critical we challenge our negative thoughts. We must rein in damaging thinking, such as, "This is too hard," and "I'm not making a difference anyway." A study conducted by Michigan State University found that the average person has 80,000 thoughts per day, 80% of which are negative.[2] What's going on? We need to change our thinking so we can change the results we get in our lives. Positive thinking will result in positive action.

The great news is, we can regain control of our thinking. We have a brilliant goal-seeking part of our brains called the reticular activating system, or RAS for short. We can program our RAS to help us achieve our goals. This part of the brain brings to our attention the things that are important to us and discards everything else.

2 Millett, M. "Challenge your negative thoughts." *Extension*, Michigan State University, 31st March, 2017. http://msue.anr.msu.edu/news/challenge_your_negative_thoughts

Because we are faced with so much information and noise every day, and we couldn't possibly take it all in, our RAS acts like a filter. We program it and it filters what we see, then helps guide what we do. So, when you think something and believe it, you make it come true. You look everywhere for evidence of it and you find it. It's a self-fulfilling prophecy.

Have you ever been guilty of focussing only on the negative? A million things could have happened in your day but you focus on the one thing that didn't go so well. That's the way you've programmed your RAS.

Let's say you think you're not the best person for a new leadership position in your law firm. If this is the way you think, you behave correspondingly. You may not speak up at the next managers meeting. You may not put the time into the application process. You might even share your negative thoughts with other colleagues, then you'll start reading into others' behaviours to confirm your thoughts. Suddenly, the email that was missed by your partner means she doesn't value your work, which means you're not important enough, which means she doesn't want you to get the leadership position. And guess what happens next? You don't get the position. You were right. You thought it, you put energy into it, your focus was purely on the negative, then bingo – that's what you got. The negative. Congratulations.

To break it down:

Thought -> energy -> manifestation.

Your thoughts are more powerful than you think. Thankfully, your thoughts are in your circle of control. You get to choose your thinking and, importantly, how you think about yourself.

CHAPTER 4.4

On my 43rd birthday, I started the day with a yoga class with my friend, Toni, the instructor. We started as usual with our warm-up, breathing exercises, downward dog and warrior pose, then it got to that part of the class I really didn't like – the headstand practice. I had never done a headstand before. I had seen other yogis in the class balance on their heads and I'd look at them and want to do it, but it just didn't seem physically possible for me. That's what I told myself.

However, during this class on my birthday, something changed. I decided to give it a shot. Toni was by my side encouraging me, talking me through it, getting me to tighten my core, helping me get my balance, and guess what? I did it.

There I was, on the mat doing a headstand. OK, it may have been for three seconds, but I've got a photo to prove it. You know the thing that changed? It was my self-talk. There was something about it being my birthday and everything else going on in my life that made me think, "Midja, you can do this. You've got this."

You may be thinking, a headstand, big deal. I get that. But for me, getting into that headstand position became super important – symbolic almost. It wasn't the physical act that mattered, it was what it stood for. For months, I had firmly believed it was something I would never be able to do, but I did it. I walked away from that class thinking, "If I didn't think I could do a headstand and I did, what else can I do? What limits have I placed on myself that I don't even realise?"

What limits are you currently placing on yourself?

Do these thoughts hold you back?

Do these thoughts impact your influence as a leader?

I remember my mum reminding me that if you can't say something nice, don't say anything at all. I think this applies firstly to what you say about yourself. If you have negative thoughts about yourself, if you talk to yourself in a damaging way, then you'll never gain the self-belief and confidence you need to achieve your goals as a legal leader. You'll only be limiting yourself.

You can absolutely transform your negative and limiting beliefs into useful, motivating beliefs – beliefs that are authentic and tap into the real you. Every time you recite those positive beliefs, you reaffirm and strengthen them. They will bring about positive action because you make it so much easier for your RAS to see evidence all around you that supports your self-belief.

Before you can become a confident leader, you must think like one. You need to create that image of yourself, the leader you aspire to be.

Simply flipping your state of mind to being more positive makes a huge difference to your success as a leader. Every morning, check in on how you are feeling. What's impacting your mood, what do you need to let go of and what do you need to focus on to turn up for your people in the best way? If you catch yourself slipping into those negative thoughts – "I'm not good enough, I'll never get that promotion" – swap them for kind, beautiful words. Be gentle with yourself.

If you do this, you'll become more appealing as a leader. You'll be approachable, consistent and, in turn, have greater influence.

CHAPTER 4.5

Let the Fun Begin

Why So Serious?

I remember something said to me early in my career as a lawyer and it has stuck with me ever since. My colleague said, "Around here, we take our work seriously – but not ourselves." I thought that sounds perfect.

You see, I'm deadly serious about my work in the leadership space, as I'm sure you are about the work you do and the outcomes you achieve for your clients. As a lawyer, your work can make a huge impact on their lives and their businesses.

But when it comes to myself? I'm not that serious.

Recently, my mobile phone rang and I answered it in my usual way, "Heyyyyyy, it's Midja." I was in a great mood that day, so there may have been a little more enthusiasm in my voice than usual. It was a potential new client calling me, an executive from a national law firm, and I think my cheerful greeting took her by surprise. She asked whether I was expecting someone else to call. I said no, that's just my phone greeting, and she laughed. It's all about creating more fun in our working day.

Now, when I talk about fun, I'm not talking about telling bad jokes or beer pong in the boardroom (although who am I to judge?). The fun I'm talking about is the approach you take as a leader and how others perceive you. Fun to me equals authenticity, genuineness and playfulness. As a leader, you'll create your own sense of fun, which will be unique to you and your leadership brand.

People rarely succeed unless they have fun in what they are doing.

DALE CARNEGIE

We all know the value of play as children. But then something happens to us when we reach adulthood and we leave our sense of play for weekends or when we're with our children. Often, we forget about playing altogether.

As adults, particularly in the legal corporate world, play is dismissed as unproductive, goofing around. We are serious people doing serious work! Well, yes, our work is serious but I believe there is still time to play and have fun.

So, why is play important?

- It stimulates your mind and your imagination, increasing creativity. You can be inventive with your solutions.

- It promotes problem-solving and the ability to adapt to situations. This is critical in this time of disruption and change. If you can't adapt, you won't succeed.

- It is a great stress reliever and boosts your happiness. Don't you want to be happier at work? Have more laughter and fun in the office?

- It increases your productivity. You will be more engaged and motivated.

- It gives you permission to try new things and the space to experiment and fail safely. You are open to other people's perspectives.

- It builds deep connections with others. It boosts comradery and builds corporate empathy. It makes you approachable and engaging as a leader.

So, my question for you is, do you make time to play every day? And what does your play look like? How we play is unique to each of us. There are so many ways to have fun and play in your work life.

Psychiatrist Stuart Brown, founder of the National Institute for Play in the US, says: "What all play has in common is that it offers a sense of engagement and pleasure, takes the player out of a sense of time and place, and the experience of doing it is more important than the outcome." Brown says that although some people may appear to be more playful than others, we are all wired by evolution to play.

Sir Richard Branson is well-known for his playfulness in business. He once said, "Try and keep bureaucracy to a minimum and remind your team that business, as well as life, should be fun."

As legal leaders, it's our job to encourage play in the workplace and become what I call "facilitators of fun"! It's time to put some play and humour back into our stressful days in the office. A survey conducted by Robert Half International found that 91% of executives believed a sense of humour was imperative for career advancement and 84% felt that people with a sense of humour did better work.[1]

I've been lucky enough in my legal career to be part of a learning and development team that liked to play and understood its value. Throughout our learning experiences, we always incorporated play, such as archery, morning walks, scavenger hunts, belly dancing, singing and even confetti cannons. All these activities were about engagement, pleasure and experiencing something different. It was about getting people out of their comfort zone and being a little silly, letting the walls down and allowing ourselves to be vulnerable. As a leader, it is vital you model this behaviour and encourage playfulness in your team. Have some fun!

As my kids often say to me, "YOLO, Mum!" You only live once, so make it count and have fun with it. Here's to more fun and play in your law firm.

---

1 "Is a sense of humour in the workplace good for your career?" Robert Half, 26th March, 2017. https://www.roberthalf.com.au/blog/jobseekers/sense-humour-workplace-good-your-career

IDEAS TO GET MORE PLAY INTO YOUR WORK:

- Think about the play you enjoyed as a child and try to recreate it. Was it something creative like painting or Play-Doh? Or did you like playing with LEGO? Outdoor play? How can you incorporate this into your day?

- Hang out with playful and fun people at work. Surround yourself with people who encourage your playful side.

- Try a new activity at work or a new way of doing something. Encourage new and crazy ideas. Think of ways to make the work task more playful.

- Be fully present. Right here, right now. It's difficult to have fun if you are continually concerned about what has happened in the past or what might happen in the future. Fun needs to happen in the present.

- Get to know yourself, then forget about yourself (more about this later). Find your place in the world. When your leadership becomes less about yourself and more about your why, your purpose and your people, you can relax and have fun with it. It's no longer about YOU.

- Build your self-confidence. If you have genuine confidence, the kind of confidence that comes from being yourself in every situation, then there is no need to be so serious about yourself. You have nothing to prove to anyone else. You can let it go.

- Finally, spend time with some little people – they know the value of play. Look at what they do. Join in and see the benefits of play and fun in your working life.

CHAPTER 4.6

Keep it Light

Let it Go

As a lawyer, the work you do can feel heavy. Moving into a leadership position can seem even heavier. No longer do you need to look after yourself and your clients, you need to look after other lawyers and their clients. It's enough to make you feel overwhelmed.

Most of us like the feeling of being in control. We like a certain degree of structure and predictability. Unfortunately, when we deal with people, things often don't go as planned. Feelings, emotions and unintended consequences get in the way. I believe the best way to deal with this is to keep your leadership light!

It's a bit like wearing a backpack. If you had to have a backpack on 24 hours a day, would you prefer it to be heavy or light? Often when I go into a meeting with a CEO or when I'm about to make a presentation, I think, "Light backpack, Midja. Keep it light and keep it playful and just be you."

CHAPTER 4.6

Whether it works out or not, whether I fail or whether I succeed, I'm still me. I'm still confident and I still believe in myself.

For a long time, I held onto things for dear life. Think white knuckles from my firm grip! I held tightly onto my marriage, my relationships with friends, my family and my job. I thought if I could hold all this down – if possible, nail it to the floor – then I would feel secure and confident. I wanted to feel in control and I thought this was the best way to go about it.

If I didn't maintain this tight grip, I felt that everything in my life would get away from me. I had a fear of losing the people and things that meant the most to me. The problem with this fear is, when things inevitably do change and the unpredictable eventuates, it's extremely hard to deal with. And in leadership, the unpredictable happens!

One of the advantages of keeping things light in your leadership role is that it allows you to have a long, strong, healthy career in the legal profession because it reduces stress and burnout. It allows you to play the long game and design a career pathway that's right for you.

If you walk into the office every day with a heavy backpack, it's going to have a physical and emotional impact on you. I'm talking about stress, worry, anxiety and depression. It's also going to impact your relationships – firstly, in your personal life with family and friends, and secondly, with the people you're trying to lead. Because in this crazy, stressful, busy, manic, volatile, uncertain and ambiguous world, people want to feel good. People want to feel like they belong, they want to feel connected. As a leader, you can provide them with this environment. But if you're stressed and heavy in your leadership, they will disengage and disconnect.

Lightness comes from prioritising your work and putting things into perspective. This gives you a steadiness and calmness as a leader. Lightness can also look loud and fun at times; the playfulness we described in the last chapter. Whatever it looks like for you, it gives your people a sense of security and they'll make a strong connection with you and what you stand for.

When you keep things light, you can be yourself. You recover quickly from mistakes and move on from disappointment. You know that just around the corner is another opportunity. You can maintain your confidence and your self-belief, even when things aren't going your way.

Being light in your leadership role doesn't mean you don't care. It doesn't mean being flippant about your work or what's going on for your team members. Rather, it means accepting what you can and can't control and enjoying what is. Sometimes, you just need to let it go. Let things be light and free. Yes, let opportunities and people into your life. Welcome them, but know they may not be there forever and things are inevitably going to change. It's the one certainty in life.

The Circles of Life[1] explain how some situations are within your control or influence, while others simply are not. Let's look at the three circles:

---

1 Chittenden, C. "The Circles of Control, Influence and Concern," *Talking About*. http://www.talkingabout.com.au/3ControlInfluenceConcern

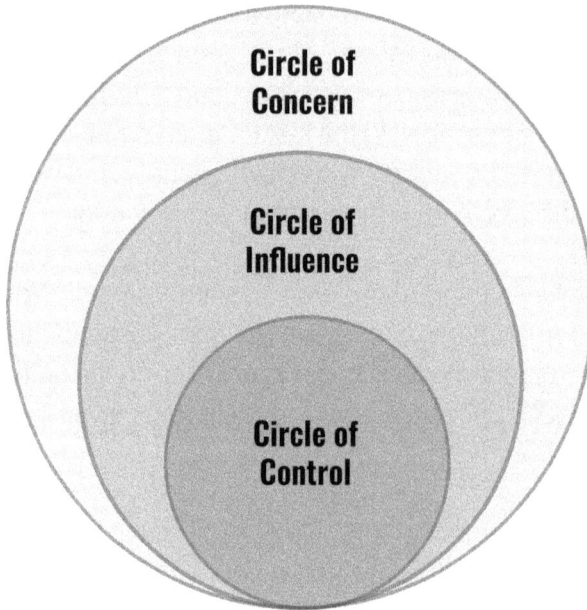

Your **Circle of Concern** includes everything that matters to you – everything you're aware of and everything that impacts your life. Some things you can influence and control, but others you can't. For example, the weather is something that has an impact on your life but you can't do anything to influence or control it. It's simply a concern. Yes, you can complain, whinge and criticise the things that concern you, but it won't make any difference. Best to focus your time and energy elsewhere.

Your **Circle of Influence** includes everything you can impact and do something about. This circle is linked to your relationships with others and the influence your actions can have on their behaviour. An example of something in your circle of influence is whether you get that next firm promotion. There are things you can do that will influence this decision but, in the end, it's not in your control. Someone else will make that decision.

Your **Circle of Control** includes everything you can directly make happen. These things are not dependant on anyone else, only yourself. It can be described this way: Control = Awareness + Choice. Once you are consciously aware of something, you have the power to make a choice and control the outcome. An example of something that is in your control is your attitude. No matter what is thrown at you in life, you choose the way you respond.

IDEAS TO KEEP THINGS LIGHT:

- Live more in the moment. Tell yourself, "This is what I can do today." Stop ruminating about the past. Consider what you can do today in your leadership role and focus on that.

- Have a real sense of who you are. Knowing your purpose and the value you bring means you won't worry so much about what others think.

- Evaluate your current relationships and commitments. Ask yourself, "How do these things feel? Are they heavy or light?" Consciously decide to spend less time and energy on the things that feel heavy. Take things out of that backpack and make it light.

- If you feel heavy and burdened by a situation in the office, determine what about it sits within your circles of concern, influence and control. Acknowledge and let go of everything in your circle of concern and plan the actions you can take to increase your circles of influence and control. Remember, you decide where you spend your time and energy.

- Live a rich and diverse life with plenty of play. Engage with others, meet new people and make time for the stuff you love to do.

Grant me the serenity to accept the things I cannot change, the courage to change the things I can and the wisdom to know the difference.

THE SERENITY PRAYER

CHAPTER 4.7

Experiment

Take a Risk

Benjamin Franklin said that there are three types of people in the world:

1. **Those who are immovable.** Won't change. Don't get it and don't want to.
2. **Those who are movable.** See the need for change. Prepared to listen.
3. **Those who move.** People who make things happen.

As a leader, it is your job to make things happen. You have to create movement, think differently and change the status quo. Leadership takes creativity.

To solve complex people and process problems, you need to experiment. There must be a "safe-to-fail" culture, where you can fail faster and learn quickly what works and what doesn't. You need to understand how and when to apply different leadership approaches while still being real and authentic.

> *When there's no experimenting, there's no progress. Stop experimenting and you go backward. If anything goes wrong, experiment until you get to the very bottom of the trouble.*
>
> THOMAS A. EDISON

When I work with a client through a leadership issue, whether it's related to a team member, their leader, a client or a process, I always take the approach of "let's keep this open, light and let's experiment".

It's like those chemistry experiments you did at school. You take a number of elements, put them together in a particular environment (for example, apply heat or freeze them) and see what reaction you get. If you change the quantity of one of the elements, the outcome will be different. If you change the environment, the outcome will be different.

Recently, I developed a nasty eye condition. Both eyes were swollen, red and itchy, and without make-up I looked like I'd aged about 10 years overnight. Not a good look!

I went to see my local GP, who has been our family doctor for nearly 20 years. He knows me very well. He asked me whether I was up for an experiment. My reply was an immediate, "Of course!" So, he gave me one cream for my right eye and a different cream for my left eye. He said, "Use these for a week, then come back and see me. Let's see what happens." I loved this!

Fortunately, both creams worked well, so I didn't end up with a lopsided face or any other ghastly side effects. But my GP's approach reminded me of the power of experimentation.

If you want different results, you have to try something different. It's about challenging the current way of thinking and asking that question, "What else is possible?" Again, you must be prepared to step out of your comfort zone in your leadership role and put on the white lab coat and protective eyewear.

Just like a chemistry experiment, sometimes you need a little more or a little less of an element. Sometimes you need to be more directive, sometimes you need to stand back and be more curious. Some situations need you to act quickly; others require a slow and steady approach. In some instances, all it takes is a change in the environment to alter the result.

So, how can you experiment more in your role to solve problems and grow as a leader?

1. Identify real-life business problems. What are your most pressing issues? They might relate to people, strategy, culture, processes or structure.

2. List all the current elements of the problem, including the environment.

3. Develop a hypothesis. If I change this, then the outcome will be this. A hypothesis will give structure to your experiment and the possible next steps.

4. Give it a go. Fail often and fail fast.

All life is an experiment. The more experiments you make, the better.

RALPH WALDO EMERSON

In today's world, you need to be a **bold thinker**. You must lead innovation and creativity in your team and organisation. By focussing on constant experimentation, you will strengthen your leadership capability and skill set, becoming a confident, courageous and agile leader. **You must not let your fear of failure or embarrassment stand in your way.** When you take risks and experiment, you are bound to have embarrassing moments. It's part of the experience.

The secret of the creative life is to feel at ease with your own embarrassment.

PAUL SCHRADER

Do you look back on something you did one or two years ago and feel embarrassed? Do you get that awkward, cringe-worthy feeling about something you said or did? Yes? Perfect!

Recently, I was mentoring a client for an upcoming presentation. I asked her about her prior experience with public speaking. She looked at the floor and said that looking back, she felt really embarrassed by the last presentation she did. She told me a little about what happened – her nerves, her stumbles, her preparation. At the time, she thought she did OK but in hindsight, there was a lot of room for improvement.

As she shared this with me, I just listened, smiled and thought, "How wonderful."

The way I see it, if you look back on what you did in the past and cringe, it means you've grown and developed. And that's something to be celebrated. If you go through your whole life with two thumbs up, no embarrassing moments and no self-talk of, "Jeez, what was I thinking?", you've lived your whole life on the one level. You've plateaued. You haven't challenged yourself or stepped out of your comfort zone.

Life is about getting out there and doing your best, knowing that your best will keep getting better!

IDEAS TO TURN EMBARRASSMENT INTO A POSITIVE:

- Connect your embarrassment with your personal growth and development. Look how far you've come!

- Remember what psychologists call the "spotlight effect". You will always overestimate the extent to which your actions are noticed by others. You need to put your actions and their impact into perspective. You remember the moment but who else does?

- Practice self-compassion. Be kind to yourself. Keep things light and playful.

- Share your embarrassing moments. They make the best stories. Researchers have found that people who display embarrassment are more prone to be liked, forgiven, and trusted than those who don't.[1] As a leader, these stories show vulnerability and authenticity and connect you with your people.

- Finally, let go of the past. You don't have to replay it over and over in your mind. Giggle at it, learn from it and move forward. Focus on what's next for you.

---

1 Keltner, D., & Anderson, C. (2000) Saving face for Darwin: Functions and uses of embarrassment. *Current Directions in Psychological Science*, 9, 187-191

CHAPTER 5

LEADERSHIP IDENTITY

CHAPTER 5.1

Discover Who You Are as a Leader

How Do You Like Your Eggs?

Recently, I was having coffee with some colleagues, talking business. It got to 10.30am and I said, "Look, I'm going to have to order something to eat. I'm starving. I'll just order some eggs." In response, one of my colleagues asked, "How do you like your eggs, Midja?" and the others started to laugh. The reference went straight over my head. I mean, what was so funny? Then she said, "You know, Julia Roberts in the *Runaway Bride* movie." I thought about the reference for a moment and remembered the 1999 romantic comedy movie starring Julia Roberts and Richard Gere.

In the movie, Roberts plays Maggie, a woman who keeps getting engaged, then runs out on her fiancés just before the wedding. Gere plays a journalist writing a story on the "runaway bride". He interviews her ex-fiancés and at the end of each conversation, he asks, "By the way, how does Maggie like her eggs?" Each fiancé gives a different response – scrambled, fried, omelette, poached. You see, Maggie would eat her eggs the same way her fiancé at the time did.

Gere's character confronts Maggie about her wedding disasters. The conversation gets quite heated and he blurts, "You're so lost, you don't even know what type of eggs you like!" Ouch.

Leadership development must start with self-development. Lasting confidence as a leader is based on a firm foundation of who you are. It's like a majestic tree that stands tall, unwavering. Its strength comes from a strong root system. As a leader, you need to develop a solid sense of self. Getting to know yourself and finding your identity as a leader can be confronting, yet the rewards are boundless.

To truly know yourself, you need to hold a mirror and take a long, hard look at yourself. Sometimes, just the thought of holding that mirror can be scary! It's like when I've had a big night out with the girls – I wake up, catch a glimpse of myself in the mirror and think, "Argh! Who is that?" My hair has succumbed to the dreaded cowlick and I have panda eyes from my black mascara. Sometimes you may not want to look in the mirror, you may not like what you see, but it's necessary if you want to gain a deeper level of self-awareness.

This deeper level of awareness is crucial when you step up into a new role and there are new expectations placed on you. It is at these times when you can second guess yourself and the imposter syndrome can develop.

If you don't put in the time and energy to get to know yourself, your tree won't develop deep roots. You'll base your self-worth as a leader on what others think of you. Your identity will come from the expectations and views of others, not from who you truly are. Your confidence will waver and you'll be constantly unsure of yourself and your direction.

You'll be like a tree that sways in the breeze from lack of strength. One minute you stand for this and the next you stand for something else. You're unpredictable and it makes it difficult for your people to follow you. They're not sure who you are and what direction you're heading in. For you as a leader, this swaying in the breeze is also exhausting.

It's likely that one of your strongest motivations will be to be liked as a leader rather than trusted and respected. Steve Jobs, co-founder of Apple, once said, "If you want to make everyone happy, don't be a leader, sell ice cream." When you're a leader, you're often forced to make the tough decisions for the firm and, ultimately, someone will always be unhappy. In these times, it is important you are trusted and respected as a leader. You may also be liked – in fact, I think it's a good start to be "likeable" as a leader – but it's important to be liked for who you truly are, not who you think your people want you to be.

Finding your identity as a leader requires you to peel back your layers to discover what's underneath. It's about discovering your personal values, beliefs, purpose, legacy and talents. All these things make you unique. They make you who you are and great leaders know who they are and dare to be themselves every day.

I've struggled at times to gain clarity on my own leadership identity and brand. I've questioned whether it appeals to the corporate market and have second guessed myself. I've asked myself, "Is anyone going to do business with someone called Midja?" Well, damn it. This is who I am and this is how I like my eggs.

My question for you is, how do you like yours?

CHAPTER 5.2

Create Thinking Space

Ask the Right Questions

As a lawyer and a leader, you're busy. It's difficult to find the time to shut out the rest of the world, switch off from the pressures of your job and the needs of your team, and just be. Add to this the busyness of your home life – housework, errands, children, partner, pets – and it's no wonder having the time to think can seem like a pipedream.

But you need to find that time. You need to sit with yourself and spend some time just with you. Make it a priority. Leaders can spend so much time "doing" that they stop "being". One of your key responsibilities as a leader is to think and plan for the future. You need to create space to do this – thinking space without the noise and distractions. Space to consider how you want to lead and what you want to focus on as a leader.

When you don't prioritise this time, when the noise and busyness of each day gets in the way, you miss the opportunity to learn more about yourself and improve as a leader. The hectic pace of life takes over and you fall into bed each night exhausted, only to wake the next morning to start the daily grind all over again – another busy day. One week turns into a month and before you know it, another year is done and dusted. You may want to spend time alone, but feel it's impossible to get that time. I've known leaders to hide in coffee shops or unoccupied offices or even work from home for a morning, to grab some quiet thinking space. There can be so many demands on your time and energy.

You can be so busy that it's easy to get distracted by other people's priorities and demands. This leaves little time for you to focus on your own personal development. Sometimes, that might be the way you like it. You can focus on everyone else but yourself and you get to avoid asking yourself the tough questions, the questions that will challenge your thinking. However, it's your answers to these questions that will provide you with valuable insight into how you can improve in your leadership role, make it your own and move towards your goals. There may be times when your answers surprise you and you think, "Where did that come from?" A real "a-ha" moment.

Thoughtful answers help you see situations differently. Your answers could change your attitude and the way you respond to a situation in the future. For example, if something went wrong in your day, perhaps you made a bad decision at work, a simple question such as, "What did I learn from today's decision?", turns a negative situation and into a positive one.

Asking questions helps you view every situation as an opportunity to learn. It's easier to identify areas that need growth and development.

Questions also allow you to examine the meaning of a situation and your response to it, so you can learn more about yourself.

The intention of self-reflection is not to be over-critical. It's not about judging yourself or blaming others or playing the victim. It's important to be insightful yet playful with your answers. Keep them light. Instead of wasting time navel-gazing and dwelling on the past, acknowledge it and use it to move forward.

Author and life coach Tony Robbins refers to these types of questions as power questions. Robbins says, "Successful people ask better questions, and as a result, they get better answers." So, it's time to think about what questions you could ask yourself to get better answers – and better results.

US author and business coach Marshall Goldsmith believes asking questions – or "triggers", as he calls them – is key to personal growth, awareness and the ability to effectively lead others. Goldsmith has a friend ring him each night to ask him a series of questions, such as: "Did you do your best today to set clear goals, preserve your client relationships or be grateful for what you have?" Marshall has done this for years and revises the questions depending on his priorities. He rates his efforts on a scale of one to 10 and ensures he's honest with himself. He calls these questions triggers because they are cues that move you forward in life, in the direction of beneficial change, particularly in a leadership role.

Asking yourself, "What did I learn today to be a better leader tomorrow?", will set you up for success. You will always be looking for ways to improve, learn and develop your attitude and skills. This behaviour, in turn, influences your people and you will create a culture of continuous self-improvement and a workplace of lifelong learners.

CHAPTER 5.2

Leaders often get caught up in the fast pace of their work environment and don't take the necessary time out to slow down. Sometimes great leadership takes consideration and restraint. As a leader, you need to regularly turn off the noise, reflect and find the calm amongst the chaos. By making self-reflection a habit and asking yourself the right questions, you get clarity on what makes you happy, what brings you joy and what you could do differently in your leadership role. It also helps you detect your purpose, your legacy and what connects you with your values.

You could set yourself reflection questions for the day, the week and the end of the year. It's important to create a ritual that works for you and ask questions that align with your priorities and direction. Your questions should be framed positively and have a useful outcome. For example, asking, "Why don't I have the confidence to speak up at a meeting?" can be reframed as, "What can I do at the next meeting to be more confident to speak up?"

Sometimes your answers will come straight away; other times, they may take a little longer. You might find it useful to use the same set of questions for a period to gain clarity and a deeper understanding of a behaviour or attitude. Record your questions and answers on paper or digitally. It's useful to look back at what you wrote a year ago to remember where you have been and how far you have come.

So, sit back, put your feet up, and ask yourself the right questions for you at this time in your life. Make it a habit and you will gain deeper self-awareness and grow your confidence as a leader.

? SELF-REFLECTION QUESTIONS:

1. What did I learn today?

_____

_____

_____

2. What was the most important thing I did today?

_____

_____

_____

3. What do I need to let go of?

_____

_____

_____

4. What am I happy about in my life right now?

_____

_____

_____

5. What am I proud of?

_____

_____

_____

6. What am I grateful for?

_____

_____

_____

_____

7. What do I enjoy doing most in my role?

_____

_____

_____

_____

8. What did I give to others today?

_____

_____

_____

_____

9. Who do I spend the most time with?

_____

_____

_____

10. Who makes me feel happy?

_____

_____

_____

11. What do I want to learn next?

_____

_____

_____

_____

12. What am I making excuses for not doing?

_____

_____

_____

13. How can I be more helpful to others?

_____

_____

_____

14. What did I do for myself today?

_____

_____

_____

15. What can I accept that I can't change?

_____

_____

_____

Quality questions create
a quality life.

ANTHONY ROBBINS

CHAPTER 5.3

Define Your Values and Legacy

How Do You Want to Make a Difference?

One of the keys to knowing yourself and having a sense of identity as a leader is knowing your personal values. Your values form your foundation.

Values are your preferences and priorities in life. They provide you with meaning and motivation. We all have them, whether we're aware of them or not. Your values help you make sense of your world and interpret your life experiences. They are personal to you and in this regard are different to morals and ethics.

Morals are principles of what is right and wrong. They are judgments, whereas values are neither right nor wrong. They simply are. Sometimes your values can seem so "right" to you that you believe everyone prioritises them the way you do. But they are only your personal values and are no better or worse than anyone else's.

Ethics are an accepted set of standards or behaviours, usually developed by a professional society within a particular profession. As lawyers, we gain an understanding and appreciation for ethics in our profession early in our careers.

Ethics govern and constrain your behaviour. Values also impact your behaviour, but two people can share the same value and be motivated to behave in a different way. For example, think about the value of family and belonging. This is usually a high-priority value for a new mum, and it is also a high-priority value for a member of the Mafia! It's safe to assume the behaviours associated with this value would vary considerably between these two people.

In the words of Paul Chippendale, founder of Minessence International Cooperative: "It doesn't matter what values you have, what matters is how you live them." As you can see from the above example, the same value can be lived in very different ways.

So, where do your values come from? They are formed by many factors, including your age, gender, education, IQ, experiences, upbringing, culture, family, peers, the environment and your work. Your values are personal and will change over time. It is likely that your values will shift as you move from the role of lawyer to the role of leader.

Each of us is driven by our values. They guide our decision making and behaviour, whether we like it or not. Your power comes from being able to move your values from your unconscious to your conscious mind. In other words, when you know what your values are, you have greater control over your decisions and direction. If your values are stuck in your subconscious, it's difficult to know why you react the way you do. In the words of Swiss psychiatrist Carl Jung, "Until you make the unconscious conscious, it will direct your life and you will call it fate." Without knowing your values, you struggle to understand your biases and view of the world.

You might ask yourself, "Why do I struggle to be motivated doing this type of work? Why am I procrastinating? Why am I reacting so negatively? Why does this new work policy push my buttons?" If we don't consciously connect with our values, we can't put into words our why, our purpose or how we feel. And when we can't do that, we fail to make our feelings known to others. Values make communication and understanding as a leader so much easier.

If you've ever had a goal you couldn't achieve, or if you've ever lacked the motivation to put in the hard yards, chances are the goal was not connected to one of your high-priority personal values. It might have been something you thought you "should" do, but because it wasn't linked to your values, there was no real drive to achieve it. It held no significant meaning for you. If you want to succeed with your goal-setting, make sure you link your goals to one of your top values.

Your values filter the way you see the world. For example, let's say an opportunity to work interstate is presented to two people. If one of them has a high value of family and belonging, they may feel anxious because it means they will be away from their partner or children. However, if the other person has a high value of financial security and the work means a wage increase, they might jump at the chance.

Your values also dictate what excites you and what bores you.

CHAPTER 5.3

When I'm in a meeting or at a friend's barbecue, I like to observe people's reactions to the conversation. As soon as someone's eyes light up or I see them get on the defensive, I know the conversation has hit one of their top values – or a nerve! You can't help but react when your values are impacted.

Another advantage of knowing your values is that it's easier to seek work projects and opportunities that connect with you. If you can align your personal values and your work, bingo! You create flow. This is when work doesn't feel like work – you're on point, you're in the zone, you can work for hours on end and you don't know where the time has gone. Have you ever felt this way? If you have, it means your work has connected with your values.

Great leaders understand their values and behave in a way that is consistent with them every single day. As a leader, your values are the key to influencing and understanding your people. Knowing your own values as a leader means you can be authentic and build trust with others. Your people know who you are and what makes you tick. They understand you. They may not always agree with you but they know why you've made a particular decision.

So, take the time to discover your values as a leader. The leading values profiling tool I use is the Minessence Values Framework. This framework consists of a set of 128 values and their descriptors, which are maintained and continually developed by an international group of experts. You can complete an online questionnaire that processes your responses to create your personalised values map, identifying which of the 128 possible values are a priority for you.

You can also gain a more informal view of your values by asking yourself questions associated with your preferences and priorities.

QUESTIONS TO IDENTIFY YOUR VALUES:

1. Think of a time when you felt completely at ease and fulfilled. What was it about the situation that made you feel like this?

   _____

   _____

   _____

2. Think of a time when someone or something irritated you and pushed your buttons. What made you feel this way?

   _____

   _____

   _____

3. If you had to move to another planet and could only take five things with you, what would they be? Why? What do those five things represent to you?

   _____

   _____

   _____

4. Considering your answers to these questions, write down what you consider to be your top five values.

   _____

   _____

   _____

5. Do you have opportunities in your career to experience these values?

_____

_____

_____

_____

6. What are these opportunities?

_____

_____

_____

_____

7. What extra activities could you add to your life to experience more of these values?

_____

_____

_____

_____

Your personal values are an integral part of who you are. As a leader, it's essential you gain a clear understanding of your values, share them with others and keep them front of mind in your everyday decision making.

Once you have identified your personal values as a leader, you can use them to connect with your legacy and purpose. This is your why. Author and marketing guru Simon Sinek says we must all start with our why. Too many of us get caught up in what we do, but the first question must always be why we do it.

Working hard for something you don't care about is called stress. Working hard for something that you love is called passion.

SIMON SINEK

Why do you get up every morning? Focusing on your legacy allows you to jump out of bed each day with energy and purpose. Through your leadership role, you'll create a lasting influence on the people, organisations and causes you are involved in, which will one day add up to something others perceive to be your legacy. Now is the time to stop and consider what your legacy will be.

Sadly, in 2017, I attended the funerals of several people close to me – including my dad's. As I stood in the church, looking around at my family and friends, listening to the stories shared during the service and later over a few beers, my heart burst with love and pride. My dad's life was a life well spent, and he left an everlasting impact on others.

CHAPTER 5.3

Later that night, when I was alone and tucked up in bed, my thoughts turned to my own funeral. I asked myself, "Would the people present have warm hearts and fond memories of me? What would they say about me and my legacy? How would I be remembered?"

When you define your legacy, you give your life purpose. You can live with a clear objective as a leader. You know who you are and what your life is about. Your legacy gives you clarity on your decision making. It helps you decide when to say yes and when to say no – something that can be tough to do in our busy lives. Your legacy makes your life choices so much easier. All you need to do is ask yourself, "Does this contribute to who I am and how I want to make a difference?"

None of us lives forever, but what does live on is the impact we have on other people's lives and the difference we make. Our legacy is the end-game. You can't take anything with you when you die; all that matters is what you leave behind.

I think all of us could tell a story about someone we will never forget, someone who changed our lives for the better, and who has, therefore, touched the lives of so many others.

For some people, the impact they make will be public and far-reaching – perhaps on the world stage. For others, like my dad, their impact will be the profound difference they make in the lives of those closest to them: their inner circle, their partner, their friends, their children and their colleagues.

The nature of your impact doesn't matter. It is personal and unique to you. What is important is that your legacy connects with your values, your priorities and what you believe in.

Defining your legacy is like beginning with the end in mind, which is Habit 2 in Stephen Covey's book, *The 7 Habits of Highly Effective People*. If you can define your purpose and the difference you want to make, you can start making your leadership legacy a reality now by putting into place congruent thoughts, behaviours and actions. If your legacy is not defined, you risk spending your time and energy on things that don't truly matter. You can end up living a life of regret and what-ifs.

Often, people don't consider their legacy until they face a life-changing event or even their own mortality. When this happens, some people look back on their lives with satisfaction, content knowing they wouldn't change a thing. Others feel compelled to make changes immediately, if they still have the opportunity. They want to ensure they say and do the things that matter, the things that will leave a lasting impact.

You can't change your past but you still have time to make the difference you want to make. You can create the legacy you want in your leadership role. It's about taking the time to define and discover what that legacy is, then committing yourself to the necessary steps to ensure it comes true. There is no time for regret.

QUESTIONS TO GAIN CLARITY ON YOUR LEGACY:

1. Imagine a banner with your name on it and three words underneath. What would those three words be?

   _____

   _____

   _____

2. It's your 10-year work anniversary at your law firm. Who is there to celebrate? What do they say about you?

   _____

   _____

   _____

3. If a movie was made about your life, what would the title be?

   _____

   _____

   _____

4. "One day your life will flash before your eyes. Make sure it's worth watching." – Gerard Way. What would feature on your life's highlight reel?

   _____

   _____

   _____

Doesn't everything die at last, and too soon? Tell me, what is it you plan to do with your one wild and precious life?

MARY OLIVER

CHAPTER 5.4

Find Your Leadership Magic

And Turn it Up!

"It is important to remember that we all have magic inside us."
– J.K. Rowling

Your leadership magic is unique to you. If you can discover it and use it to its full potential, you can live your values and leave your legacy.

Your magic will contribute to your greatest strength as a leader. It will be what you're known for. Your magic will captivate others and build your reputation and leadership brand. It's the gift you have to share with your people.

It reminds me of the story of the Disney fairies. As you might know (particularly if you have young children), there are different types of fairies in Pixie Hollow. There are water fairies, animal fairies, light fairies and tinkers − fairies who like to make and fix things. The most famous fairy of all, of course, is Tinker Bell − with her blonde hair, blue eyes, emerald green dress and rebellious nature.

Tinker Bell's problem was that she didn't want to be a tinker fairy. She fought against it all the way. She desperately wanted to be a different type of fairy. She looked at the other fairies, saw what they did and wanted to be like them. She envied them. She didn't realise she had her own unique gift.

She tried her hand at other fairy skills but no matter how much she wanted to succeed, she continued to fail. You see, Tinker Bell had a talent, a skill, a magic inside her she couldn't fight. She was a tinker. Tinkering was her gift to the world.

Now, Tinker Bell was determined and tenacious. Once she accepted that she was a tinker, she decided to bring her own unique style to the tinker role.

It's the same with your leadership magic (or your talent, natural skill, strength, whatever you want to call it). You can make it your own. If you fight against your magic, it feels unnatural. Leadership becomes hard. You feel that you're wasting your time and not moving forward but you're also not sure what you're supposed to be doing. It gnaws at you. You know there is something more you must give, but you don't know what it is. It's your job to find that magic.

I've mentored leaders who, like Tinker Bell, have tried to fight their natural skill, their magic. One female leader had a real gift for attention to detail. She was a perfectionist by nature. She could pick up an error, conduct a SWOT analysis and assess a situation for gaps like no one else, but she hated her talent and thought it was boring. She believed anyone could do what she did. But they couldn't. For her, it was innate. Whether you want to argue for nature or nurture or a combination, it doesn't matter. She had a gift. So, my advice to her was to embrace her gift and make it her own. She needed to bring her personality and her brand to it, just like Tinker Bell.

Sometimes, your magic will find you. It's easy to recognise and identify. But sometimes, it's hidden deep inside and only the right circumstances or opportunity will bring it out. Finding your magic may mean trying new things and seeing what feels right, particularly when you're starting out in a leadership position.

If you think about the leaders in your current firm or leaders you have worked with in the past, you will discover that they all had their own unique magic. Something that made them different from everyone else. What's your difference?

? QUESTIONS TO DISCOVER YOUR MAGIC:

1. What do people in your organisation and team come to you for? Is it for your positivity, empathy, decisiveness, humour, attention to detail, determination, bravery or reasoning? Perhaps it's a skill such as writing, speaking or selling. Whatever it is, pay attention to it.

_____

_____

_____

_____

2. What comes naturally to you? I like to call this the "duh" moment. It's that thing you do, say or feel that you think is easy. It's something you think everyone does. But guess what? It's not what everyone does. It's what you do. It's so natural to you that you don't even have to think about it. You don't realise it's your magic. You may not place any value on it because it doesn't take much effort. It's time to take notice of this talent and not ignore it.

_____

_____

_____

_____

3. What do you love doing? What's the best part of your day? What's that thing you do at work that doesn't feel like work? I hear people say they would continue to do a certain type of work or an aspect of their job even if they didn't get paid for it. What is this for you?

_____

_____

_____

_____

_____

4. What excites you? What gets your adrenaline going? What do you look forward to? There might be some anxiety and fear around it, but it's that mixture of excitement and fear you need to recognise.

_____

_____

_____

_____

_____

CHAPTER 5.4

So, what's your magic and how can you use it to become a leader worth following? In fact, not just use it but amplify it to become extraordinary.

When I open my eyes each morning, a message stares back at me in a white frame with beautiful gold writing. It says, "You did not wake up today to be mediocre." Each morning, I read that message and say to myself, "No, you did not." And neither did you.

Leaders often ask me, "Should I spend my time focusing on my magic, my strengths, the things I'm already good at? Or should I try to improve my weaknesses, the gaps in my skills?" My answer is to always play to your strengths.

To me, it comes down to this. **You can either be ordinary at everything or be extraordinary at something.** If you focus on your weaknesses, you may become well rounded. People often think that's a great thing. They put their energy and focus on improving their weaknesses to be a jack of all trades. However, you've got to ask yourself, "Do I want to be described as well-rounded or extraordinary?" I know which one I want to be.

If you play to your strengths, you can become extraordinary. The most inspiring leaders are known for something. They know their ace card and they know how to use it. They make sure they play to their strengths because they know that in doing so, they make the biggest difference in the lives of others.

To be a great leader, you need to focus on your magic. You need to give it all the energy it deserves. You must amplify it and dial it up. I'm talking high definition!

Of course, you need to be aware of your weaknesses and find ways to contain them but your time as a leader is best spent doing what you do well.

Malcolm Gladwell, in his book *Outliers*, refers to the 10,000-hour rule, based on the research of Herbert Simon and William Chase. According to this rule, it takes 10,000 hours – in other words, a lot of time and practice – to become proficient at a complex task.

If it takes that much time and effort to become exceptional at something, don't waste it on things that will make you mediocre or average. Keep the spotlight on your strengths, where you are centre stage and where you shine. When you play to your strengths, you take the lead. Why would you step away from centre stage to make room for something you're not good at, something you don't enjoy and doesn't come naturally to you? The spotlight shines brightest when you do your best work, the work you're meant to do, and contributing in the most meaningful way possible. This is where you will make the greatest impact on your people.

At a young age, I knew I loved to talk. I remember the joy that came from my show-and-tell days at school. It was my favourite time of the week. While my friends dreaded getting up in front of the class, I was nearly wetting my pants with excitement. This love of presenting stayed with me and grew.

When I was a lawyer, I took every opportunity to present anything at any time to anyone. In addition to managing a law office and servicing my clients, I would facilitate, train and present. I was part of the learning and development team, without officially being part of the team. I presented at team meetings, firm strategy days, Law Association days, induction courses, anything. Why? Because I wanted to get to that 10,000 hours of facilitating and speaking.

CHAPTER 5.4

I knew it wasn't going to happen by accident. I had to be deliberate about it.

In other words, if you don't actively seek opportunities to amplify your strengths, you'll never fully discover what you're capable of. Imagine what's possible if you stopped focusing on your weaknesses and gave your full focus to strengthening your magic, your gift. Think about what you could achieve.

The great news is you have more resources at your fingertips now than ever before to practice and hone your talent: online courses, TED Talks, public workshops, podcasts, research papers, YouTube clips, the list goes on.

A mentor is another highly valuable option. A mentor is someone you aspire to be in your field of expertise. They've been there, done that and bought the T-shirt! They are inspiring and extremely knowledgeable. You can learn a lot from your mistakes but you can learn a lot more from the mistakes of a mentor. My own mentors have been amazing sources of knowledge and motivation. Who do you admire and aspire to be? Reach out to them and ask whether they would be willing to take you under their wing.

Remember, the greatest impact comes from amplifying your talent. As a leader, when you use your strengths to make a difference in the lives of your people, they'll forgive you your weaknesses. In fact, they may not even notice them.

So, give your magic your full focus and attention. Give 100%. I say if you're going to do something, do it big. Go the whole way. Don't settle for good enough or mediocre – strive to be extraordinary.

QUESTIONS TO HELP YOU AMPLIFY YOUR MAGIC:

1. Firstly, what are your strengths? (see "Discover Your Magic" questions above.)

_____

_____

_____

_____

_____

2. What do you currently do to develop your strengths?

_____

_____

_____

_____

_____

3. How much time per week do you invest in developing them?

_____

_____

_____

_____

_____

4. What further opportunities can you explore to play to your strengths?

_____

_____

_____

_____

_____

5. Do you have a mentor or coach to challenge you and hold you accountable?

_____

_____

_____

_____

Focussing on strengths is the surest way to greater job satisfaction, team performance and organisational excellence.

MARCUS BUCKINGHAM

CHAPTER 5.5

Seek Feedback

Don't Care What Others Think of You? Maybe You Should (Just a Little)

We've discussed at length in this chapter the importance of deepening your self-awareness and self-perception to find your identity as a leader. But what's also important is the perception and viewpoint of others – your colleagues, clients and the people you lead.

Don't care what others think of you? Maybe you should (just a little).

What do other people hear, see and, most importantly, *feel* when they are around you? What do others genuinely think of you?

I have the wonderful opportunity to meet some amazing people in various leadership positions. It always intrigues me to hear them explain how they feel *on the inside*. To hear them talk about their self-perception, who they are, their values and beliefs and what they do for their clients. As they talk, it's hard for me not to compare their self-perception to my perception of them *from the outside*.

It's like the iceberg analogy. You know what's going on under the water, your internal feelings, but others around you have a much better understanding of what's going on above the water, your external presentation. They have a better view.

I'm not backwards when it comes to sharing with people what I consider to be their "magic". As I've discussed, I believe everyone should understand their strengths and talents and have the opportunity to dial them all the way up. However, for most of us, our cognitive blind spot (that part of ourselves we fail to see due to our own biases) gets in the way of seeing all that we are.[1] We can't get a realistic view of what's on top of the water.

American psychologist Carl Rogers said that genuine self-awareness can be honed if we take the time to join our own self-awareness (who we think we are) with the perception of what others see in us.[2] In other words, if we join what's above the water with what's below it. The idea is to fully understand yourself, you need the perspective of others. This perspective gives you the belief and mindset to become your ideal self, the very best version of you – that authentic, genuine, confident leader!

So, how do you do this?

---

1 Vazire, S. and Carlson, E. "Others Sometimes Know Us Better Than We Know Ourselves," *Current Directions in Psychological Science*, 15th April, 2011. https://journals.sagepub.com/doi/abs/10.1177/0963721411402478

2 Rogers, C. (1959). A theory of therapy, personality and interpersonal relationships as developed in the client-centered framework. In (ed.) S. Koch, *Psychology: A Study of a Science. Vol. 3: Formulations of the person and the social context*. New York: McGraw Hill.

You need to open your heart and mind to receiving feedback from others. You need the confidence to accept their gift of insight, good and bad.

Often when I give positive feedback to others, they get embarrassed, avoid eye contact, lean back and mumble something like, "I'm not sure about that," or, "Do you really think so?"

When someone gives us a compliment, we usually reject it in one of three ways. Response number one is the put down: "What do you mean the presentation went well? I completely fumbled over the start." Response number two is the deflection: "No, I thought Tom's presentation last week was much more succinct." Response number three highlights our inner sceptic (especially as lawyers): "Really? You think so? I'm not so sure."

Do any of these responses sound familiar? I know I've heard myself say them. It's time to stop! Think of positive feedback as extra nourishment for your leadership confidence. Accept a compliment with grace and allow it to reaffirm your strengths and add to your personal leadership brand.

On the flip side, when I give negative feedback, often the recipient gets defensive. I know I can do the same when I receive it. I remember a training co-ordinator coming up to me a few years ago to give me feedback on some assessments I had marked. She felt that some of my marking was inconsistent. Before she could even finish giving me the feedback, I made excuses and blamed others. She then backed away and said sorry. She apologised for trying to give me honest feedback — feedback I needed about my lack of attention to detail. A few hours later, what I had just done kicked in and I apologised to her.

Sometimes we don't want to hear feedback. It's tough, it's personal. But if we ever want people to be honest with us again, we've got to suck it up and listen, really listen, with the intent to understand.

To get honest feedback that helps you and contributes to your leadership identity, you need to do the following:

- **Ask for feedback.** Be proactive. Don't sit in your office, waiting for someone to knock on your door. The old saying that no news is good news doesn't apply to the assessment of your leadership skills. You must make asking for feedback a habit. Do it every week.

- **Be specific when you ask.** Asking someone how they think you're going in your role or slipping in the question, "So, do you have any feedback for me?", at the end of a conversation or a meeting is ineffective. You're not going to get anything worthwhile from that. It's too safe. Instead, ask for something specific. For example, "In our weekly meetings, I've been conscious that I do most of the talking. I'm keen for these meetings to be collaborative, to get everyone's opinions. Can I get your feedback after the meeting this week about how I went with it and if you felt everyone had the chance to contribute? Thanks." You'll find people will be willing to give you more honest, helpful feedback with this approach.

- **Really listen to the feedback.** If it's negative feedback, don't interrupt with your BEDtime story of blame, excuses and denials (see below).

- **Acknowledge feedback and take action.** Thank the person for their feedback, positive or negative. Make them feel valued for taking the time to give you their opinion. Ask for further clarification if you need to gain a deeper understanding, then consider whether there is any action you need to take as a result of the feedback. Think of it as an opportunity to learn more about yourself and grow as a leader.

BEDTIME STORIES

Often when we make a mistake or receive negative feedback, we react immediately and bring out our BEDtime stories:

- **Blame.** The greatest game on earth is the blame game. It was the CEO, the board, one of your team members, the admin staff, the client, etc. It was anyone's and anything's fault but your own. When things go wrong, you can panic and start to throw people under the bus to take attention away from your own culpability.

- **Excuses.** You can come up with a million and one excuses why something hasn't gone to plan. Some of them can be valid reasons. Bad stuff happens to good people. Often as a leader, we use a lack of resources as an excuse: "I didn't have enough people/time/money to make it happen." But is this taking ownership of your actions and your leadership role?

- **Denial.** You can hide the mistake and pretend it didn't happen. You can sweep it under the carpet and move on – that is, until someone else finds out about it!

BEDtime stories can be a default response when you feel under threat and out of control. They are an almost instinctive reaction to protect yourself. But what's the impact of these BEDtime stories? Ultimately, they destroy trust in your relationships. No one is going to follow a leader they can't trust.

CHAPTER 5.5

As a leader, asking for regular specific feedback is essential. It's part of the gig and a habit that must be practised regularly. The wonderful by-product of asking for feedback is that you develop relationships based on honesty and trust.

CHAPTER 5.6

Take Off Your Armour

Be Vulnerable

Once you've done the work on discovering who you are as a leader, it's time to show yourself to your people. This means having the courage to be vulnerable. When you know who you are and you can be who you are, leadership feels light, it feels purposeful.

I've mentored lawyers who have shied away from sharing too much of themselves, saying, "It's not about me, it's about the firm." As discussed in Chapter 3, lawyers score low on the trait of sociability.[1] Some lawyers would much rather spend time working alone on a client file than working with people and sharing who they truly are. They prefer to be in their corner office and when they do have to face their people, they hide behind a firm-branded

---

1 Leeke, S. "The Importance of Developing Leadership in Law Firms," Thomson Reuters, 24th July, 2014. http://insight.thomsonreuters.com.au/posts/importance-developing-leadership-in-law-firms

CHAPTER 5.6

PowerPoint presentation with figures, projections, matrixes, graphs and other "inspiring" material.

Guess what? Your people don't care about that stuff. What they care about is the person standing in front of them. There is no room to hide as a leader. My advice is that if you want to hide, don't go into leadership. As a leader, it is all about you; not in an egotistical way, not for personal gain or to become a rock star. But as a leader, you believe in something passionately, you want to create change and to do that, you need your people to follow you. People won't follow you unless they feel connected to you. They need to understand you. To be a leader worth following, you must open yourself up and be vulnerable.

When I discuss vulnerability with leaders, often the discussion turns to whether this is a sign of weakness or strength. Strong leadership is traditionally viewed as tough, competitive, goal-oriented, rational and linear. But is this always the case? Can't strength be the opposite? Instead of fighting, instead of putting up walls, isn't it strong to let the walls down and have the courage to be vulnerable? Can't strength be associated with collaboration, emotion, passion and empathy?

Research professor Brené Brown, in her book *Daring Greatly*, says: "Vulnerability is not weakness, and the uncertainty, risk, and emotional exposure we face every day are not optional. Our only choice is a question of engagement. Our willingness to own and engage with our vulnerability determines the depth of our courage and the clarity of our purpose. The level to which we protect ourselves from being vulnerable is a measure of our fear and disconnection."[2]

---

2 Brown, B. *Daring Greatly: How the Courage to be Vulnerable Transforms the Way We Live, Love, Parent, and Lead.* Avery Publishing Group, 2015.

To show yourself to your people, to be authentic and genuine, you must be vulnerable. The courage to be vulnerable comes from truly knowing yourself, your values, your beliefs, your purpose and your legacy. If you don't do this, it's like wearing a coat of armour. When you are unsure of yourself, when your self-worth and self-esteem come from the need to be right (that traditional view of strength), you put your armour on for protection. You don't want to be hurt. You don't want people to judge you or see the real you.

Without your armour, you feel exposed. You fear you'll get taken advantage of. You fear you'll be judged or rejected. This is a huge risk when your confidence has been built on what other people think of you instead of what you think of yourself. I know that when I walk into some law firms, I get the feeling everyone is wearing a coat of armour, ready for battle.

As a leader in a law firm, the battles can seem relentless. You feel you must fight for your voice to be heard, fight for resources, fight for recognition and fight for your team members. You head into meetings wearing your coat of armour because it gives you strength. It makes you feel invincible. Now, imagine that everyone else at the leadership table is wearing their coat of armour, too. How does it feel? When everyone wears their armour, there is no opportunity to connect. You bump against one another in a competitive way. It slows everyone down. It stops you from being agile. You can't see the real person under the armour and everyone looks the same.

It's time to take the armour off. You don't need it. Your power comes from your authenticity, by knowing yourself and being yourself. When you take the armour off, you'll feel lighter. You'll feel more like you. People will be able to see the real you and connect with you as a leader.

CHAPTER 5.6

The great thing is that once you take your armour off and become vulnerable, other people at your firm will feel safe to do the same. What a different leadership table you'll be sitting at! When everyone takes off their armour, you can connect with one another, see one another, really listen to and understand one another. You might have different points of view, but you will use this diversity to create synergy and innovation, not competition.

Now, before you start sharing your deepest, darkest secrets in the meeting room, let me clarify that being vulnerable doesn't mean you should share *everything* with *everyone* all the time. It's about being true to yourself.

Sometimes you may not want to share or feel the need to share. There might not be enough trust in the relationship yet or it might not be the right situation. And that's OK. You can still acknowledge your feelings and beliefs to yourself even if you don't outwardly share them. It's also important to always check your intention for sharing. Is it to connect with your people or to prove your point of view?

THE SPECTRUM OF SHARING

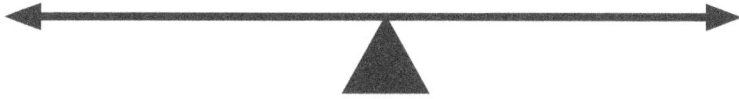

UNDERSHARING	AUTHENTICITY	OVERSHARING
Disconnection, Distrust	Connection, Trust	Disconnection, Distrust

- **Undersharing.** This is when the armour is on. It's a bit like wanting to tap on someone's chest and ask, "Hello, who's in there?" At this end of the spectrum, people feel they don't know the real you. Because you reveal so little, people suspect a hidden agenda and there is scepticism about your ability to lead. People will be unable to make an emotional commitment to you as a leader because they don't know who you truly are. There's disconnection and distrust.

- **Oversharing.** At the other end of the spectrum, when you share too much too early, it makes people feel uncomfortable. Oversharing and sharing for all the wrong reasons creates doubt about your leadership motives and makes you appear self-absorbed and ego-driven. "It's all about me." The result is the same: disconnection and distrust.

- **Authenticity.** Then comes the sweet spot in the middle. This is where you can be open, honest and vulnerable in an appropriate way. This is where you build high trust with others and make a real connection.

CHAPTER 5.6

Great legal leaders share who they are with their teams in an authentic way. You will never feel so strong as you do once you take off your armour. You can be vulnerable and you can be real. You don't need a coat of armour to protect you, you have something better: your confidence.

Every interaction you have, every conversation you engage in, is a chance to show yourself and build a real connection. It's about assessing each situation.

? QUESTIONS TO ASK BEFORE SHARING:

1. Do I feel safe to show my true self?

_____

_____

_____

_____

2. What's my intention in sharing my opinion, belief, feelings or story?

_____

_____

_____

_____

3. Am I sharing to build trust and connect with and serve others?

_____

_____

_____

_____

4. Or am I sharing to prove I'm right and feed my ego?

_____

_____

_____

_____

In order for connection to happen, we have to allow ourselves to be seen, really seen.

BRENÉ BROWN

CHAPTER 5.7

Create Your Leadership Brand

Be Visible

Everything you have explored in this chapter about leadership identity contributes to the creation of your leadership brand. It tells your story and sets you apart from others.

Your brand is the way other people see you. It's what you're known for and what you represent. As Jeff Bezos, founder and CEO of Amazon, says: "Your brand is what others say about you when you're not in the room." It's comprised of your ideas, your values, your expertise and your style. To be memorable, it needs to be distinctive, visible and consistent.

When you create a strong leadership brand, it gives you influence. It opens opportunities for you and the people you lead, allowing you to make a bigger difference and scale up your expertise and ideas.

CHAPTER 5.7

This is more important now than ever. Why? Because by 2020, more than 50% of the US workforce will be self-employed.[1] It's safe to say Australia will see a similar trend. This means that as a leader, you need to set yourself apart from the competition. In other words, to lead with influence, you need to sell yourself. To cut through the noise, you need to market your skills and talents through a strong brand.

Be your brand's designer. Don't let it develop by default. If you don't act now to brand yourself, others will on your behalf. You will be judged purely by what others say about you. It's up to you to show the world who you are through what you say and do.

Your brand is a personal promise to your people. It tells them what they can expect from you. In a leadership role, you need to keep this promise and exceed expectations to build trust and commitment.

The most important thing to remember about your brand is that it must always be based on your authentic self. Start with your values, beliefs, purpose, magic and legacy. All the elements we have explored in this chapter of the book are needed to create a brand that is congruent with your character and who you are at a roots level.

If you try to build a brand without doing the work on yourself first and without a deep level of self-awareness, you can destroy the trust others have in you. People can detect when your brand is fake. You may be able to pretend to be someone you're not for a while, but you won't be able to sustain it. It's too hard. Your behaviour will be inconsistent and unpredictable, and you will struggle to live up to the brand you try to portray, letting people down.

1 Rashid, B. "The Rise Of The Freelancer Economy." *Forbes*, 26th January, 2016.
https://www.forbes.com/sites/brianrashid/2016/01/26/the-rise-of-the-freelancer-economy/#4496dbdd3bdf

Be steadfast and know what you stand for. You must act according to your purpose, strengths and expertise. At some point in your career, people will get to know the real you. This usually happens when you are faced with a challenging time. It's easy to maintain appearances when the sun is shining, but once the storm hits, your character is exposed. At this point, if your character doesn't match your brand and who you say you are, you will lose the trust of your people and your influence as a leader.

Of course, your brand will evolve. It needs to, because your values and priorities will change. Your personal brand will become stronger and more distinctive as you gain greater insight into your purpose and who you are as a legal leader.

IDEAS TO CREATE YOUR BRAND:

- **Tell your story.** Authentic storytelling is a huge part of building your brand (more about storytelling in the next chapter).

- **Consider what you say yes and no to.** Where you spend your time says a lot about what you value.

- **Your outward appearance impacts your brand.** Be deliberate about how you dress, how you look, how you walk and how you talk.

- **Align your online personality with your brand.** Be consistent with your message on social media and be cautious about what you "like" and share.

- **Let your personality shine.** People want to know the real you. They want to know what's underneath the suit (see Chapter 5.6 – Take Off Your Armour). What are your interests outside of work? I've known leaders who love surfing, who are coffee fanatics, who are foodies, who adore their miniature schnauzers or who cycle every day to work. Share these passions with your people.

- **Make every interaction count.** Everything you say and do adds to your brand.

Think about what you can do every day to build your personal brand so it is congruent with who you truly are. The most important thing is that your brand is visible, which means you must be visible as a leader.

I work with professionals who are at different stages of their careers. I have the privilege of working with young graduates who are at the start of their professional careers, building their presence in their firm and profession. I discuss with them the importance of being visible and creating their authentic leadership brand.

I also work with executives. I remember mentoring a leader who reported directly to the CEO. The interesting thing was that even at that stage in his career, we discussed the same thing: how to be visible. This leader was driven and passionate about his work. He worked crazy hours and put in 100%. However, the feedback he received was that he needed to give more. His reaction? "I'm not sure I have anything left to give."

In this situation, it's not about giving more. It's about being smart with your focus, time and energy. Of course, delivering on your operational goals is vital to your success, but "business as usual" is a given. You can keep your head down and work extremely hard but if no one knows what you're doing, you and your team won't get the recognition or future opportunities.

It may be a lack of confidence that stops you from promoting yourself and your team. This is when you don't have enough self-belief to speak up and acknowledge your hard work and achievements. It may feel safer to keep your head down and stay under the radar. You may be so busy and overwhelmed with work that you feel you don't have the time to "get out there". It's not a high priority. Or it may be that you fear criticism and judgement from others if you speak up. This harks back to the tall poppy syndrome, which is still alive and well in Australia.

However, increasing your visibility is not about bragging or over-the-top self-promotion. It's about building your personal leadership brand and the reputation of your legal team so you can be of greater service to others.

IDEAS TO INCREASE YOUR VISIBILITY:

- **Do work that adds the greatest value.** Ask yourself: How do I add the most value to this organisation? What am I getting paid to do? What is my expertise? What is my magic? Focus on that. Effectively delegate work to team members and administration staff and get clear on your role. This may require you to extend trust to others and let go of any perfectionist tendencies.

- **Use your voice at every opportunity.** Speak up in meetings. Demonstrate your knowledge and share your opinions and ideas. Consider the agenda prior to meetings and think about questions to ask or examples to share. Volunteer to represent your team at company events. Work on your presenting skills and gaining more confidence if you need to. Ask to be placed on high-visibility projects.

- **Build connections with influential people.** Expand your network within your organisation and externally. Build relationships across different departments. Make the time to attend events and have your elevator pitch ready. Speak with your immediate manager regularly. Grow your online connections and contribute to your online community.

- **Participate in learning opportunities.** Commit to your own professional development. Set an example to your team members. Attend internal and external learning sessions and workshops, ask questions and meaningfully contribute to discussions. Give valuable feedback. Help others' learning and development – give a webinar, mentor a junior team member, write a blog post.

CHAPTER 5.7

Increasing your visibility is about making sure people understand what you do, how you contribute and what makes you unique. Without visibility, you will get lost in the crowd and fail to develop your own authentic, strong leadership brand.

Think of your leadership as a business. If you don't market or advertise or have any signage out the front, what would happen? You would go out of business. You might be the very best at what you do but if no one knows about you, you won't get any work. It's the same with leadership. You need to market yourself to attract and retain your best people.

So, build your leadership brand. Get out there and be seen.

The power of visibility can never be underestimated.

MARGARET CHO

LEADERSHIP SKILLSET

CHAPTER 6.1

Remove Your Cape

Now Forget About Yourself

"Before you become a leader, success is all about growing yourself. When you become a leader, success is all about growing others."
– Jack Welch

Spending time and energy on yourself is the greatest gift you can give to your people. It's important you really get to know yourself, get into the leadership mindset and establish your leadership identity. Once you've done this work (as outlined in chapters 4-5), you can shift your focus to your people. In other words, you have to get to know yourself first, then forget about yourself.

With a strong leadership identity, you can widen your focus to your legal team, your law firm, the legal profession and the greater community. You can consider how to use your magic to influence and inspire others into action.

In your role as a lawyer, you spend most of your time as an *expert*. You are valued for giving the right advice. You may have to step in and *rescue* other team members at times when deadlines are approaching and client demands are high. As a lawyer, there is often very little time for *coaching others*. Your billable hours are one of the key measurements and this means keeping your head down and working on client files.

But as you transform from great lawyer to great leader, your time and focus must change. You will still need to play all three roles of expert, rescuer and coach, but the majority of your time needs to be in the coaching space.

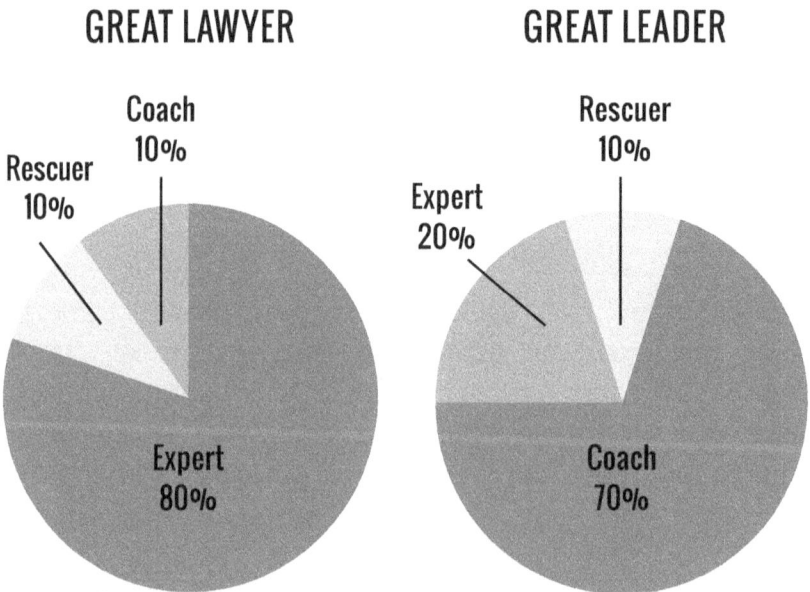

GREAT LAWYER   GREAT LEADER

GREAT LAWYER
Rescuer 10%
Coach 10%
Expert 80%

GREAT LEADER
Rescuer 10%
Expert 20%
Coach 70%

THE EXPERT

The leader who plays the expert tells their people what to do. They give the answers. When you're busy and have limited time, it is tempting to fall back into the role of expert as a leader.

However, telling people what to do reinforces dependency. This can be appealing to a new leader. You create a dependency to serve your own needs. You think, "If they depend on me, then I'm needed, I'm valued." But when you put too much focus on being the expert, your people don't need to think for themselves. This results in limited learning and growth, which is bad news for your firm and your own development as a leader. They turn into "yes" people who blindly follow your instructions.

The role of expert can be a tough one to relinquish as a legal leader. It's like going to the gym and only working on one muscle; your expert muscle. Over the years, that muscle develops and grows. It feels comfortable to work that muscle, it's strong. But when someone asks you to work on another muscle, it feels strange and it's hard work!

THE RESCUER

I met with a colleague recently and we discussed her leadership style. As she talked, it became clear she was a rescuer. I said, "So, you wear a cape and your undies on the outside of your pants? You're the superhero in the office, right?" She nodded and laughed. I laughed, too, because I've been that superhero leader.

As leaders, we can easily fall into the role of rescuer. Some of our people may be really comforted having a superhero they can call on day or night. It's like living in Gotham City and putting out the bat signal, then sitting back, acting helpless and waiting for Batman to arrive. He always does.

So, what motivates the superhero leader? I think their intention is positive. They want to help others and get the job done. Obviously, there's a payoff for saving the day. You feel needed, indispensable. It's good for the ego. However, the impact is similar to that of the expert leader. You end up building a team of people who are reliant on you. No resilience, no growth, no development, no accountability. When things go well, they look up to you and sing your praises but when times are tough, you know who they're going to blame, right? You. And you've created that "victim" paradigm.

THE COACH

Great leaders are great coaches. It's as simple as that. Coaching develops the capability and talent of your people. It cultivates their confidence and self-leadership.

It can feel a little scary stepping into the coaching space if you haven't spent a lot of time there before. If you haven't ever worked that muscle in the gym. There is a fear around relinquishing the safer roles of expert and rescuer, which you know so well. You may have great experience in these roles, but they will not serve you well as a legal leader.

So, it's time to remove your cape and coach your people. Be there for them, guide them, support them, but let them make mistakes and fail, too. Leadership is all about the long game. No short-cuts.

CHAPTER 6.2

Take Centre Position

Leadership is a Contact Sport

Recently, I was coaching a leader who had received some off-the-cuff comments from his team members. He had walked into a meeting and one of his team members said, "Hello, stranger." Ouch!

Another senior leader commented to me a few years ago that when he walked into the room at an annual firm event, people gasped. They were so shocked to see him in the flesh.

As a leader, if you get these reactions from your people, it's time to re-think your priorities. Leadership is a contact sport. You've got to be in there. It's not about putting on a suit, catching a lift to the top floor, walking into a corner office and shutting the door. Remember, sociability is a low-scoring trait amongst lawyers (see

Chapter 3). However, as a legal leader, you must get comfortable with getting up close and personal with your people.

Face time in business is priceless. And not just business, but in all relationships.

The word company, as in a "companion", comes from the Latin word for bread, "panis", meaning "to share bread".[1] The daily luncheon habit of US oil industry magnate John D. Rockefeller is described in the biography, *Titan*. Every day, Rockefeller would sit down with his people, have lunch and talk. This was how he built strong, sustainable relationships.

In order to succeed as a leader in the legal profession, you need to gain commitment from your people to deliver outstanding results to your clients. Your people need to be willing to go the extra mile. You need to persuade, inspire and influence and you can't do this through a computer screen or telephone line. Leadership needs face time.

As a mentor and facilitator, I sometimes work with my clients on the phone or via Skype, but nothing beats the connection I make when I'm face-to-face with a client, either one-on-one or in a workshop setting. When we can see one another, when we can see each other's faces, reactions and body language, we can deeply engage with one another. When we're face-to-face with someone, our "mirror neurons" mimic the other person's behaviours, sensations, feelings and energy. Our brains love it. Rapport is quickly established and communication is easy.

---

1 "Breaking Bread with 'Companion'," *Merriam-Webster*. https://www.merriam-webster.com/words-at-play/history-of-word-companion

As a leader in a busy law firm, life can get hectic and you become transactional with your people. It's easy to forget to make time for them and to just postpone that meeting for another day. The result? Your people disengage, disconnect and stop performing at their best.

It's time to lead from centre position.

In 2010, I attended a learning and development conference in Orlando, Florida, called Learning 2010. My colleague and good friend Debbie and I had been invited to speak about our firm's residential training facility and the courses we designed and facilitated. It was an amazing opportunity and one of my all-time favourite experiences.

On the second day of the conference, we headed out for our lunch break and enjoyed a meal with our fellow delegates, not knowing what was going on inside the auditorium. We were soon to find out. When we opened the doors to commence the afternoon session, we were shocked. During the lunch break, the entire Orlando Philharmonic Orchestra had set up in the middle of the room and started playing! The beautiful sound resonated around the auditorium.

The conductor of the orchestra was Roger Nierenberg, author of the leadership book, *Maestro: A Surprising Story About Leading by Listening*. Roger invited us to hear the orchestra from out in front, where the conductor traditionally stands. He then asked us to experience what it was like to listen from the middle of the orchestra. What a different feeling! A richer, stronger sound. I felt more connected, like I was part of the music.

Leadership is a lot like conducting an orchestra.

CHAPTER 6.2

As a leader, you can spend all your time out the front of your people, waving your hands around, giving directions. A little more of this, a little less of that. Of course, direction and instructions are needed in leadership but what is also needed is connection, understanding and knowledge of what is *actually* happening in the business, not just what's written in the latest board report.

How do you experience these things? How do you get information? You need to get amongst it, get in the centre. From the centre, you will gain a different perspective. You will be closer to the business processes, the clients and, of course, your people. From the centre, you can easily access every part of the business and everyone in it.

If you only ever stay out front and never get amongst your people, you can lose perspective of what's really going on in your law firm and in your team. You lose touch with reality. You get caught up in the executive hype and talk the good talk: "We have strong cultural alignment with our values, we have a dedicated and motivated workforce ..." Blah, blah, blah. All the rhetoric in the world. You can get caught up in your own management report and start believing it. You rely on your positional power, become completely task-oriented and forget about your people, who are your greatest asset.

IDEAS TO GAIN CENTRE POSITION:

- **Get out of the top-floor corner office and be seen.**
  Engage in conversations. Ask questions and listen.
  Usually, the more senior the leader, the further they are
  physically away from their people and the "hub" of the
  business. At my old firm, the managing partner and I
  would often sit and have a cuppa in the kitchen. It was
  amazing how much he heard and what he learnt from
  the people coming in and out of the lunch room, talking
  away, not even noticing the managing partner was
  sitting at one of the tables.

- **Make time to attend events.** Turn up to other team
  meetings and events – for example, a celebratory
  morning tea, induction training for new staff or a lunch-
  time webinar. At first, people might be shocked to see
  you. They might even be a little anxious or concerned.
  It's important you're open and honest about your
  intention for attending. It might take a little while to
  create a new cultural norm.

- **Bring your people physically together.** When you're
  meeting, training and learning with others, it's not just
  the formal discussion in the room that's valuable. It's
  also the conversations you have at morning tea or
  lunch. This is where the real magic can happen. You
  engage in a conversation with someone that sparks a
  new way of thinking and you build relationships with
  people you would never have met otherwise.

I've experienced this as a facilitator and as a participant. During my career as a lawyer, I was lucky enough to attend numerous training and strategy events in Australia and overseas. The bonds I made with my fellow colleagues will last a lifetime. With every experience, my connection, loyalty and commitment to the firm grew stronger. Now, as a facilitator at team-building and leadership programs, I continue to observe the interactions and conversations between participants. I can feel their connections growing.

Great leaders focus on long-term effectiveness, not short-term efficiency. Yes, in the short-term it costs money to bring people together, but the long-term benefits of retention, engagement and performance outweigh these costs. As a leader, you need to believe in your people, invest in them and put them first.

Sure, webinars, Skype meetings, emails and e-learning have their place. They are wonderful tools to connect people with just-in-time learning concepts and compliance training, and they help managers stay connected when they are geographically dispersed. However, when it comes to cultural alignment, leadership development, behavioural change and inspirational connection, you need to bring your people together. Those things can't happen over a screen.

- **Discover the client experience.** Get up close and personal with your clients. Attend a client meeting or site inspection, whatever you can do to connect with your clients and understand their needs.

So, as a leader who is busy conducting your orchestra from out front, remember to take the time to move into centre position and discover the richness of the music.

CHAPTER 6.3

Seek to Understand

Slow is Fast

As a lawyer, you like things to be logical. You like to have a precedent to follow. However, when it comes to people leadership, things can sometimes seem illogical.

A certain approach may work for one person but not with another, or maybe not even with the same person in a different situation. This can be frustrating and leave you second-guessing your effectiveness as a leader. It's the reason why the attitude of lightness, playfulness and curiosity we spoke about in Chapter 4 is so important.

You must always remember that people do things for *their* reasons, not *yours*.

CHAPTER 6.3

When I think about my children, my flesh and blood, I birthed them, nurtured them, spend every day of my life interacting with them, yet they still see the world differently to me. Sometimes I sit at the dinner table with my three and think to myself, "Who are you people and where did you come from?"

Now, think about what happens in the workplace. As a leader, you are trying to influence people who you've perhaps just met. You probably know little about their background, upbringing and values, but you expect them to see the world as you see it. They don't, and this is actually a great thing. This diversity of viewpoints brings about innovation and creativity, if you embrace that diversity as a leader. It's difficult to know what your people think and help them lift their performance unless you take the time to listen to them. A great leader listens and genuinely tries to understand others' points of view.

One of the greatest needs we have as human beings is to feel understood, as though someone "gets us". Our children want to be able to share their ideas, feelings and opinions without fear of being judged. They want to be accepted for who they are. And guess what? So do the people you lead in your law firm.

When you consider the rapid changes occurring in the legal industry as discussed in Chapter 1, it's not hard to understand why your people might feel anxious and uncertain in their roles. As their leader, it's your job to listen to them and provide certainty, confidence and direction.

Once your people feel understood, once they have been listened to without judgement or agenda, they will be open to listening to you. They'll feel valued for their unique contribution and will want to contribute to the success of your team and your law firm.

They'll trust you and be loyal to you. It's only from this position of mutual understanding that you can genuinely inspire, engage and motivate your people.

So, what gets in the way of effective listening?

You have so much going on operationally day to day in your role, you may feel you don't have the time to listen. Sometimes in a new leadership position, you want to impress and get "runs on the board". You want to bring about change and get noticed. Maybe this is driven by the fear that if you don't prove yourself quickly, "they" are not going to think you're up to the job. This fear drives your behaviour as you try to prove your worth and you forget to take the time to truly listen to your team.

Lawyers are known for their sense of urgency and efficiency.[1] These traits are good for adversarial work, but not so good for leading people. As a leader, you need to slow your pace and take the time to understand what is going on for your people and what they need from you to perform at their best. This takes courage and strength of character. You need to have the right mindset as described in Chapter 4. You need to listen and gain a deep understanding of your people's issues, then you'll be in a position of influence.

You see, from deep understanding comes influence. Influence doesn't come from a title or a position, it comes from understanding your team as a whole and each team member individually. It's the same with any relationship. Good luck trying to influence a teenage son if he doesn't feel understood. You might get lip service – in other words, compliance – but you'll never get commitment.

---

1 Richard, L. "Herding Cats: The Lawyer Personality Revealed," LawyerBrain.
http://www.lawyerbrain.com/sites/default/files/caliper_herding_cats.pdf

IDEAS FOR EFFECTIVE LISTENING:

- **Check your mindset and intention.** Do you want to understand the other person or merely get your own point of view across? Remember, it's their story, not yours. Keep an open mind. Stay curious. Leave your assumptions and biases to one side. As soon as you start judging, you compromise your effectiveness as a listener and leader.

- **Give them your full attention.** Make sure you face them and maintain eye contact. In most Western cultures, eye contact is considered a basic element of effective communication. A lawyer once told me that when she was typing away on her computer and one of her team members came into her office, she had a simple ritual: stop, turn and smile. I like this. Remember to set aside papers, books, your phone and other distractions. Make the person feel valued.

- **Be aware of non-verbal cues.** A person's body language and facial expressions can give you a real insight into their true feelings, sometimes even more so than their words. Watch for any incongruence between their words and what their body tells you.

- **Practice empathy.** When listening to someone talk about a problem, refrain from suggesting solutions. If they want your advice, they'll ask for it. Show you understand where the speaker is coming from by reflecting the speaker's feelings. "You must be excited by the new project," or, "I can see that you're feeling confused." If the speaker's feelings are hidden or unclear, occasionally paraphrase the content of their message back to them. Sometimes a simple nod shows your understanding. The idea is to give the other person proof that you're actively listening.

- **Allow silence.** Most of us feel awkward when there is silence. Don't be tempted to fill silence with your own words. If you allow the silence to just be, often the other person will continue to open up. Some people need time and space to gather their thoughts, particularly if they're talking about an emotional issue.

- **Ask for clarification if needed.** Of course, when you don't understand something, you should ask the other person to explain it to you. But rather than interrupt, wait until they pause, then say something like, "I didn't understand what you just said about ..."

If you work on your listening skills, you are destined to be a better, more compassionate leader.

Listen, or your tongue will make you deaf.

NATIVE AMERICAN PROVERB

CHAPTER 6.4

Coach for Performance

The Gift of Feedback

Feedback should be a gift of information for your people. It's a means of letting them know what they are doing well and how they can become more effective. When feedback is about improving performance, it creates strong relationships.

As a leader, you want to promote open and direct communication. Problems arise when leaders are unsure how to structure their feedback or start the conversation. If you don't put the time and effort into giving effective feedback and having coaching conversations, it can demotivate your team members.

So, how can you give effective feedback?

- You must first be open to receiving feedback, as discussed in Chapter 5.5. If you as a leader can't handle receiving feedback, how can others accept it from you? In the words of Brené Brown, "If you're not in the arena getting your ass kicked, then I'm not interested in your feedback."

- Give feedback based on first-hand knowledge if possible. Structuring feedback on what you have observed directly, rather than on what someone else has told you, will make the conversation easier.

- Even if the feedback is negative, approach the conversation as a positive opportunity to remind your team member of your expectations and to gain commitment from them.

- Be specific and give examples. Feedback such as, "You're doing a great job," is too general and doesn't provide your team member with any details. What exactly do you want them to continue doing? What is contributing to the "great job"?

- Avoid using "but" or "however", as this will undermine your key message. No feedback sandwiches, either – this is where you say a positive comment, then a negative one, then finish on a positive note. People will only take away what they want to hear and ignore the rest.

- Be future-oriented. Describe what would make a difference in the future, not just what went wrong.

Your people will be more willing to accept feedback if you are fair and consistent. Above all, you must show them respect.

Curiosity, which we discussed in Chapter 4.1, is one of the most important attributes of a great legal leader. So, it's important that during your feedback conversations, your assumptions and prejudices are left at the door. A question I always find helpful in any feedback and coaching situation is, "What do I know for sure?" It's also the title of one of my favourite books by Oprah Winfrey.

I remember facilitating a workshop early in my career and noticing one woman in the group. She made no eye contact with me the entire day. She didn't crack a smile, not even at my funniest of stories (and I'm pretty funny!) and she hardly wrote a thing in her workbook. She ignored my instructions and spent most of the day doodling and daydreaming.

I couldn't believe it. What had I done wrong? She obviously didn't like me or what I had to say. She wasn't interested in any of the content and thought it was a complete waste of time. I drove home from that workshop feeling frustrated, deflated and disheartened.

The next week, as part of the course, I had scheduled one-on-one debriefing sessions with each participant. As you can imagine, I was dreading the phone conversation with her. However, the funniest thing happened when I made the call. Before I could say anything, she apologised. She told me about an argument she'd had with her long-term partner on the weekend before the workshop and she was questioning whether they had a future together. She said her head wasn't in the right place that day and, in hindsight, she probably shouldn't have come along.

The lesson I learnt from that experience was to always ask myself, "What do I know for sure?"

In this situation, I had quickly climbed the Ladder of Inference. The Ladder of Inference explains how you can move from a piece of data (a comment made or something you have observed) through a series of mental processes to a conclusion.[1]

THE LADDER OF INFERENCE

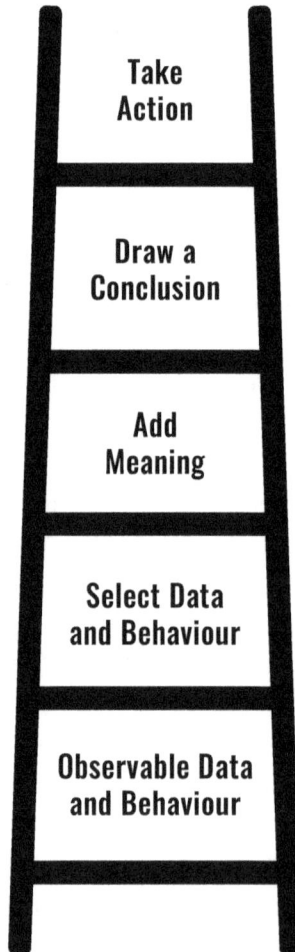

Take
Action

Draw a
Conclusion

Add
Meaning

Select Data
and Behaviour

Observable Data
and Behaviour

---

1 "The Ladder of Inference," MindTools. https://www.mindtools.com/pages/article/newTMC_91.htm

In my example, I selected observable data from the participant — namely, no eye contact, no smiling and no writing in her workbook. I quickly added meaning to the data — she's disengaged and not interested. Then I drew a conclusion — she doesn't like me or anything I have to say. Was my conclusion correct? Not at all.

When I coach clients, I often find the same flawed reasoning in their conclusions. We can see or make up issues all around us and, of course, sometimes they're correct, but more often than not, there is something else going on we're unaware of.

We don't see things as they are,
we see them as we are.

ANAIS NIN

The Ladder of Inference can be dangerous because it happens extremely quickly. You can be oblivious to the fact you're only selecting some of the observable data. This means you act and give feedback based on only part of the story. Nobody else sees your thought processes or knows what stages you have gone through to reach your conclusions. All they see is the action you take as a result, and this can undermine your effectiveness as a leader.

How can you stop yourself from climbing the Ladder of Inference?

1. Firstly, accept that you are always going to draw meaning and inferences from what other people say and do. It's natural.

2. The key is to be aware of this process and test your assumptions instead of blindly accepting them.

3. Ask your people more questions about what they are thinking. Practice empathic listening and seek first to understand.

4. The quickest way to go back down the ladder, to challenge your conclusions, is to ask that simple question: What do I know for sure?

The skill of giving effective feedback is essential to your role as a legal leader. You should see every conversation as a coaching opportunity. Remember, coaching is about looking forward. Your feedback should move your people from where they are now to where they want to be and help them put the steps in place to achieve it.

As a leader, you need to ask the right questions to empower action and expand your people's thinking. The right question can change the way a person views a long-standing belief. It can shift their mood or reveal a possibility they had never considered before. Ask open-ended questions when you want to evoke expanded thoughts and ideas and stimulate creative thinking. Ask closed questions when you want to seek commitment from a team member, particularly at the end of a coaching conversation when actions have been agreed upon.

A helpful model for coaching conversations is the GROW model. This model was developed in the 1980s by business coaches Graham Alexander, Alan Fine and Sir John Whitmore.[2] I have used this framework for many years with my coaching clients and it works. It's simple yet powerful four-step process that will keep the feedback conversation on track.

---

2 "The GROW Model of Coaching and Mentoring," MindTools. https://www.mindtools.com/pages/article/newLDR_89.htm

G – GOAL	What is the goal of the conversation? What is your objective? State the goal clearly at the start of the conversation. Sometimes, the goal might simply be to make the person aware of their behaviour and its impact and nothing more.
R – REALITY	Explore the current situation. Listen empathically to their point of view, as discussed in Chapter 6.3. Acknowledge what you hear. As the leader and coach, ask questions to get your team member to open up, e.g. What's missing? What's working? What obstacles are in the way?
O – OPTIONS	What options can the team member think of that will create progress? Explore all the alternatives. Now is the time for brainstorming and creative thinking. Listen to their ideas before asking whether you can share yours.
W – WAY FORWARD	Help your team member develop their action plan by ensuring they have identified all the resources needed, who needs to be involved, timeframes, obstacles and how they will overcome them.

CHAPTER 6.4

By using the GROW model to structure your feedback, you will enhance your team's performance and create awareness and commitment. Your coaching conversations will improve the confidence of your people, increase accountability and, ultimately, help you achieve your goals.

As a legal leader, you want to create a culture of feedback in the moment. Get out there and share your feedback with your team members and be open to receiving it yourself. This is the only way we all learn and get better at what we do.

CHAPTER 6.5

Speak to Inspire and Connect

Communicate Until They Mock You

Communication is vital to your role as a legal leader. It's so much more than the transmission of information. The messages you communicate help to connect and inspire your people.

Of course, communication must flow in two directions. We've discussed the importance of listening as a leader in Chapter 6.3. Now it's time to discuss the importance of speaking and clearly communicating your leadership messages. It's vital you understand your audience when you deliver a message so it hits the mark with your team members.

You must consider, what is your message and how are you going to say it? Consider your mode of communication, your words, tone of voice, facial expressions and body language. Human beings are intuitive and your people will constantly read and react to your non-verbal cues. How do you project yourself to others? Do they see you as a confident and optimistic leader or tentative and worried?

Your communication must be open and transparent. Transparency builds trust. Show your people you have nothing to hide. Be authentic in your communication style and be willing to reveal more of yourself so your people can see the real you. If you fail to do this, it undermines your effectiveness as a leader.

It is also important you communicate important messages as quickly as possible. The last thing you want people in your law firm to do is play the game of Chinese whispers. Rumours can spread quickly and if you don't communicate important information or key decisions quickly, your people will fill in the gaps with their own assumptions. There will be doubt, speculation and suspicion instead of trust, commitment and collaboration.

I recently worked with a law firm that had made the decision to cancel an annual event. They cancelled the event with the hotel, then took some time to figure out how to best communicate their decision to their people. But before any communication could be made, lawyers had already started contacting the hotel to book accommodation, only to be told by hotel staff the event was no longer going ahead. Ouch!

Your communication also needs to be consistent. As a leader, it's easy to assume that if you say something once, your people will remember it and act on it. This assumption can get you into trouble. If you have children, you'll understand what I mean! I often find myself saying, "How many times do I have to tell you to (insert instructions here)." If I ask my teenage daughter to clean her room or put her dirty clothes in the laundry, do you think she does it the first time? Not a chance.

I was once given the advice by a well-respected mentor that, as a leader, I should communicate my message until people start to mock me. In other words, until they start to laugh, roll their eyes like they know what's going to come out of my mouth next and say things like, "Oh well, here she goes again."

You see, it's only at the point where your people start to mock you that you know they've taken your message on board. Your message has permeated into the culture of your team and your firm and it's now part of the common language. You can then take a step back and decrease the frequency of your communication because your people will start to act on these messages. They will be your message ambassadors, with your messages front of mind, influencing their decisions and actions every day.

In a law firm I worked for, we had a set of three values that were communicated at every opportunity: in meetings, training sessions, on the intranet and they were a part of all firm policies, manuals and performance criteria. These values were communicated everywhere. I'll be able to recite those values for the rest of my life.

Your key messages need to be front of mind so your people act upon them. You want to ensure your messages are programmed into their reticular activating system (RAS). As explained in Chapter 4.4, the RAS acts as a filter for our brains. It makes certain things part of conscious thought and you want your key messages to be part of your people's conscious thinking. You want them to keep coming back to those messages in their everyday interactions with clients and other team members. They must fully understand what is expected of them.

CHAPTER 6.5

The impact of this type of communication is that you will get the desired behaviours and results you want. And, as your people grow and develop, they'll take something different away from your messages. They will adapt their understanding depending on what's happening to them at that time, their own growth and development and their specific needs. How many times have you read or heard something once, taken a couple of key points away, then a year or two later, you've come back to the same message and suddenly have a slightly different interpretation? Your people will do the same with your key messages.

If you make the mistake of thinking you can communicate something once and your people will immediately understand and act on it, you'll end up frustrated and disappointed. At some point, you will realise you've been on different wavelengths. You're not getting what you asked for and key goals are not being met.

You might shy away from repeating your message because you feel you're nagging people. Let's face it, no one wants to be labelled a nag. But without repeating your message, it won't stick. What you must do is get creative with how you deliver your message. How can you deliver your message multiple times through different media to get it across? Think about what you can do in face-to-face communications, through emails, the intranet, in meetings and the stories you tell.

So, how much is enough? How many times do you need to communicate your messages? Advertising research indicates that people show a preference for an idea or message if they are familiar with it. This is called the Mere-Exposure Effect and is a term coined by psychologist Robert Zajonc. It means that repeating a message more than once leads to familiarity with that message, which then leads to a preference for it. Studies have shown that mere exposure reaches its maximum impact between 10 and 20 exposures. After that, the effectiveness declines.[1]

Of all the leadership responsibilities, communication is the most powerful and enduring – especially in times of challenge and disruption. If you can get it right, you'll connect with and inspire your people to go above and beyond.

---

1 Relojo, D. "How Do Companies Use the Mere-Exposure Effect to Attract Customers?" *Psychreg*, 28th December, 2017. https://www.psychreg.org/mere-exposure-effect/

IDEAS TO ENSURE YOUR MESSAGES HAVE MAXIMUM IMPACT:

- Determine your big messages. For example, your vision statement, your mission, values, key client behaviours, a team charter, sayings and quotes that epitomise your key beliefs.

- Be pro-active and strategic with your communication. Create and implement a communication plan.

- Weave your messages into your storytelling. Explain the why behind your messages (more about this in Chapter 6.7 – Be a Culture Creator).

- Get in front of your people. Convey your messages in everyday conversations.

- Be mindful of your non-verbal cues. Your facial expressions and body language can affect what you want to convey.

- Look for opportunities to put your messages in written communication. For example, the firm employee handbook, emails, intranet and training documents.

- And just when you think they've got it, say it again!

CHAPTER 6.6

Discover Their Talents

Empower Them

In 2007, a social experiment was conducted in the metro train station in Washington DC. A musician played the violin for about 45 minutes and, during that time, thousands of people entered the metro. However, only a handful of people stopped to listen for a while. About 20 people gave him money but continued to walk at their normal pace. The musician collected $32. When he finished playing, no one noticed and there was no applause or recognition.

No one knew this, but the violinist was Joshua Bell, an acclaimed classical violinist and one of the most celebrated musicians in the world. He had played one of the most intricate pieces ever written on a violin worth $3.5 million. Days earlier, people had paid to see Bell perform at Boston's Symphony Hall – it was a packed audience.

CHAPTER 6.6

But at the metro, people were too busy, too distracted, too rushed to appreciate the amazing talent right there in front of them.

As legal leaders, we are also busy. Let's face it, every hour is rush hour for a leader! The pace is go, go, go. And the higher you climb the corporate ladder, the faster the pace. You sprint to catch that next train, oblivious to anyone or anything around you.

Often, you don't make getting to know the people who are new to your organisation a priority. You're too busy. At the other end of the spectrum, you may ignore long-standing employees, assuming you already know them and their strengths.

We can be quick to judge people and pigeonhole them, which means we fail to notice their growth and development, their new capabilities. All of us are continually learning and we need new experiences and challenges to keep us stimulated and engaged.

One of your key responsibilities as a leader is to identify the talents of your people and nurture and reward these talents. You play a critical role in facilitating their learning and development. Make it easy for them to grow their self-awareness, knowledge and expertise. If you can focus on the development of your people, you will build a team that is engaged, committed and performing at its best. A CEO I once worked with told me he believed his job was to find out what people were good at and let them do it. I love this!

So, how can you identify and nurture the talents of your people?

- **Slow down.** I know you want to make that next train but slow the pace. Agility and speed are great when it comes to processes – when you need to try and fail things quickly to find out what works best – but when it comes to your people, as we discussed in Chapter 6.3, slow is fast. If you rush, you will miss out on discovering and leveraging the talent you have in front of you.

- **Be inquisitive.** Find out more about the people who work with you – their values, purpose and strengths. What are their goals? What turns them on? What do they want to learn next? Then, ask questions that will challenge them. Get your people to see their problems and obstacles in a different light and open their minds to what else is possible. No one learns much from being told what to do.

- **Create connection.** As a leader, it is your role to connect your people with the law firm's vision and purpose. Get them to understand *why* they do what they do, how they contribute to the firm's purpose and what they can learn to increase their influence and impact.

- **Create the right learning environment.** You want your people to be in flow; to have just the right amount of stretch and challenge to experiment, grow and learn. Too much stretch and they'll feel anxious, stressed and burnt out. Too little stretch and they'll lose their mojo and disengage. It's important your people are intrinsically motivated to learn. You need to create a culture of learning in your firm that encourages and rewards those who seek personal and professional growth

Once you have discovered the talents of your people, it's time to give them meaningful work that allows them to use these talents to their full potential. Let them shine! Take a step back and get out of their way. Let them find their own solutions and methods and, of course, let them fail (tough, I know). It's important to empower your people to make their own decisions.

CHAPTER 6.6

I once worked with a leader who was passionate about her job. She was a perfectionist, driven and dedicated, which, of course, are all great qualities. But the flip side was that she was overprotective of her ideas, she tended to micromanage her people and it was hard to get anything out of her department. She wanted to make every decision and check every piece of work herself. There was no doubt she acted this way because she cared so much about the work and wanted everything to be perfect. But although her intention was great, her impact wasn't.

Something needed to change. Otherwise, this leader was going to suffer burnout. Her personal leadership brand was suffering. She was working long hours but getting negative feedback. However, this feedback gave her the opportunity to consider the responsibility and accountability of her team members. She realised she was scared of letting go. "What if something goes wrong?" she asked me.

This fear often holds us back from empowering our people to make decisions. As leaders, we need to make sure we have the right people doing the right things in the right way. We simply don't have the time or headspace to make every single decision in our teams. As a leader, you need to elevate your thinking.

When you empower your people to make their own decisions, it frees your time. You can focus on strategy and the areas where you add the most value. Furthermore, each team member gets more clarity on their role and level of authority. It gives them a path for career progression, which can help you with succession planning.

Empowering your people makes your team agile and fast. It builds trusts and increases creativity and innovation because you allow new, fresh ideas and approaches to the work.

When I'm in a leadership role, I like to ask my people, "What would you do if I wasn't here? What decision would you make?" By asking these questions, you step out of the role of expert and rescuer and into the role of coach, as we spoke about in Chapter 6.1.

If you retain all the decision-making power, your people will continue to be micromanaged. You'll make them dependent on you. This might secretly be what you want but it doesn't allow them to learn and make mistakes, and you won't find out what they're capable of achieving. It holds your talented people back from making the impact they could make. It also covers up unsatisfactory performance.

Of course, the risk of empowering your people is that things might not get done *your* way. Perhaps they won't get done at all or your people will fail. But they're the risks that you, as a leader, must take.

Micromanagement also costs money. According to a *Harvard Business Review* analysis, US companies are wasting more than $3 trillion on excess bureaucracy and management every year.[1]

When I speak to leaders about accountability and decision-making, I often come back to the Decision Tree model from Susan Scott's book, *Fierce Conversations*. This is a simple model for delegation and accountability. I ask leaders to think of their team as a tree and consider their team's root, trunk, branch and leaf decisions. Each decision can affect the health of their "tree".

---

1 Hamel, G. and Zanini, M. "Excess Management Is Costing the U.S. $3 Trillion Per Year," *Harvard Business Review*, 5th September, 2016. https://hbr.org/2016/09/excess-management-is-costing-the-us-3-trillion-per-year

DECISION TREE

LEAF

Make the decision, act on it, not necessary to share it.

BRANCH

Make the decision, act on it, report on it.

TRUNK

Make the decision, report before action, then act on it.

ROOT

Share the decision-making process, act on it as a team. These decisions are strategic and could cause damage if poorly made and implemented.

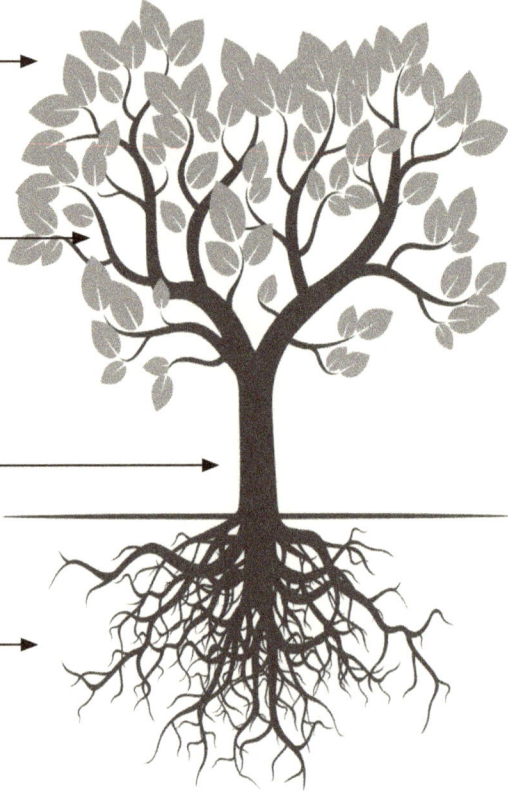

There are four categories of decisions:

1. **Leaf decisions.** Make the decision and act on it. There's no need to report the action taken. There's no real risk here.

2. **Branch decisions.** Make the decision, act on it, then report the action daily, weekly or monthly. There might be some risks associated with these decisions, but they can be mitigated.

3. **Trunk decisions.** Make the decision but report it before action is taken. There could potentially be a high risk of harm to the project, team, client or to the firm.

4. **Root decisions.** Make the decision with input from others. There could be a great risk of harm to the project, team, client or firm if these decisions are poorly made.

The analogy is that if you take a leaf off a tree, the tree won't die. In the same way, a leaf decision that's poorly made won't impact your law firm. But if a wrong action is taken at root level, it could cause serious damage to the tree and even kill it. So, as a leader, you need to determine where each decision sits, which involves some risk analysis, and communicate this to your team.

Here are some steps you can take to empower your people to make decisions:

1. Explain the Decision Tree concept to your team and make sure they understand it.

2. Ask your people to draw your team's current tree. Where are most of the decisions being made? Are you, the leader, being a roadblock to the decision-making and the agility of the team?

3. Clarify the leaf, branch, trunk and root decisions of each team member and give them clear working examples.

4. Clarify with other departments within your firm who they need to go to in your team for what.

5. Keep the Decision Tree front of mind. Maintain your intention to empower your people and be fast and agile in your decision-making. Use this language in your team.

Every hour in a law firm is peak hour. But as a leader, you need to slow your pace. Look up, engage and discover the extraordinary talent in your law firm.

? QUESTIONS TO DISCOVER MORE ABOUT YOUR PEOPLE:

1. What are the talents of each of your team members? What magic do they bring to your law firm?

_____

_____

_____

_____

2. Do your people find meaning and purpose in their work?

_____

_____

_____

_____

3. Do they understand the "why" behind their work duties?

_____

_____

_____

_____

4. What motivates each team member?

_____

_____

_____

5. What do they want to learn next?

_____

_____

_____

_____

6. What have you done to show them their value and the significance of their contributions to the firm?

_____

_____

_____

_____

7. When was the last time you made it possible for your team to be proud of their work?

_____

_____

_____

_____

8. How often do you celebrate the impact your people have on the firm's success?

_____

_____

_____

_____

9. What are you doing to make work rewarding and inspiring for your people?

_____

_____

_____

_____

10. What does a great day look like for your team?

_____

_____

_____

_____

CHAPTER 6.7

Create Culture

Build Your Tribe

Great leaders are culture creators. But what is culture? To me, this can be answered by asking two simple questions:

1. What are our values as a firm and what do we believe in?
2. What do we say and what do we do, as a result of those values and beliefs?

By answering these two questions, you can define your firm's culture. Every organisation should have a defined culture – a set of values and beliefs and a set of behaviours around those values.

The best way to truly understand a culture is to feel it, to see it, to hear it. A great example of this is to head to your local shopping centre.

CHAPTER 6.7

Picture this. My 15-year-old son and I walk into a City Beach surf and street-wear store. Now, upon crossing that threshold, I immediately know I don't belong there. These are not my people. I think, "Slowly back away, Midja." The music, the layout, the brands, the language, the people ... argh! Then I look at my son, who is smiling, relaxed and finding what he needs. This is his place and his people. What a wonderful, well-defined culture.

It's the same with law firms. I think all of us have worked somewhere and felt like we didn't belong. Then, you walk into another firm and think, "Yes, these are my people. This is my tribe." Culture is tribal. It's about our need to fit in and belong. As anthropologist Michael Henderson says, "We may have left traditional tribal settings back in the deserts but the instinct to tribe is still strong." And that's why people stay in a law firm and perform at their best. They do it for the tribe and you have a huge responsibility as the tribal leader.

There are three key aspects of cultural leadership:

1. Discovery and alignment of firm values
2. Ritualisation
3. Corporate storytelling

DISCOVERY AND ALIGNMENT OF FIRM VALUES

Just like your own personal values, which we discussed in Chapter 5.3, your firm's values will give you and your people meaning and motivation. Values are preferences and priorities.

Firm values make leading your people easier because they offer simplicity and clarity. A strong set of values reduces the need for HR policies. People simply know what's acceptable and unacceptable behaviour. If they get it wrong, the tribe will let them know. Firm values give everyone a solid foundation from which to make the tough decisions. If you're ever unsure about what to do, go back to the firm's values.

It is often the case that law firms have a beautiful plaque on the wall, sometimes in the foyer or boardroom, which lists their company values. It's glossy and shiny and takes pride of place, which is fantastic, I love seeing that. It's a wonderful cultural artefact, on one condition: that it's *true*. The values written on that plaque are what someone should feel, see, hear and experience if they started working there tomorrow morning.

Because if they aren't true, the relationships you build with your people will be based on a lie. You will recruit based on a lie. And every time your people walk past that plaque or hear the CEO or a leader in the firm talk about those values, they want to call BS.

If you're going to put your values on a plaque for all your employees, visitors and clients to see, you had better be real about what they mean and you had better live them every single day. Otherwise, you break a promise. Not a great way to build trust.

Remember, values aren't right or wrong. One value isn't better than another. You need a set of values that are aligned with the leaders of your law firm and your strategic goals. For example, for some companies, creativity and innovation are highly valued and needed, but in others, they aren't a priority. And that's OK. For other organisations, their values might be sharing and listening or equality and accountability. You don't need to pretend to value something that you don't.

If you get your values right, people will join and stay with your firm based on reality. You will have an organisation that is aligned, engaged and performing at its best. And when your people walk past that values plaque, they will feel a sense of pride, loyalty and belonging.

RITUALISATION

Rituals bind a tribe. They give your people a common experience and something to look forward to. They also give them certainty in an uncertain world.

Recently, I had lunch with a friend who told me that the firm she worked for had a Christmas tradition where every person would receive a small gift. This Christmas, however, the firm had decided not to follow the tradition. The assumption was that the decision was based on financial reasons but nothing was actually communicated. People felt disappointed, like their hard work during the year wasn't appreciated or valued.

You see, traditions and rituals are an integral part of an organisation's culture. The more meaningful rituals you have in your law firm and in your team, the stronger your culture will be. And of course, a strong culture equals strong performance.

❓ QUESTIONS ABOUT YOUR RITUALS:

1. What rituals do you have in place?

_____

_____

_____

_____

2. What things do you do in your organisation, daily, weekly, monthly, six-monthly and yearly?

_____

_____

_____

_____

3. How do you acknowledge birthdays and service anniversaries?

_____

_____

_____

_____

4. How do you celebrate the achievement of goals?

_____

_____

_____

_____

5. What is the rhythm of your meetings – i.e. how often are they held and what do you do at the start and end of your meetings?

_____

_____

_____

_____

6. When do you get your whole organisation or team together and what do you do?

_____

_____

_____

_____

There are so many opportunities to develop and embed your firm's culture and live your values. You don't have to organise huge events; often, it's the small things that make a difference. It's the coffee run, it's the birthday card signed by the team, it's the weekly meeting that always starts with a new client story.

Think about the meaningful rituals you can put into place that align with your company values and the culture you want, the culture you need, to reach your strategic goals.

CORPORATE STORYTELLING

People have been telling stories since the dawn of time. Strong cultures throughout history have shared their beliefs and values through stories, some of which have become legends that are passed from generation to generation by their leaders. If you want to have influence, make storytelling part of your leadership toolkit.

We have stories to tell, stories that provide wisdom about the journey of life. What more have we to give one another than our 'truth' about human adventure as honestly and as openly as we know how?

RABBI SAUL RUBIN

CHAPTER 6.7

For example, as a young lawyer, I was told about the importance of client care. I was informed of the steps I needed to take to build a rapport with the client, how to address the client and how to conduct an interview, and I thought, "Blah, blah, blah ... yeah, yeah. I've got it. Client care. It's important."

Then one of the partners shared with me a story. He said that one stinking hot day, he had to see a new client and his wife on their property west of Toowoomba. When he arrived, it was hard not to notice the mess inside the house. Dishes were piled in the sink and the kitchen benches were untidy. He sat down at the kitchen table to talk to the client when he noticed a cake in the middle of the table, baked by the wife especially for him. The icing was melting off the cake and it was covered in flies. I asked the partner, "So what did you do? Did you eat the cake?" The partner looked me in the eye and said, "Of course I ate the cake. You always eat the f****** cake."

Lesson learnt. That story was told to me more than 15 years ago and I still remember it. I remembered it every time I dealt with a client during my legal career, the words "eat the f****** cake" ringing in my head.

After hearing that story, there was no doubt in my mind what was expected of me and what was meant by client care and rapport. No manual, training session or 10-step instruction guide could have told me more than that one simple yet powerful story.

When you give people instructions and information in a standard way — e.g. by telling them what is right or wrong and what you want them to do — it's often filed away, never to be retrieved again. They may have some fleeting interest in what you're saying but there is no change in their knowledge or behaviours. They have no meaningful connection with what you're saying.

However, people react to stories and narrative in an entirely different way. We process stories through immersion – by putting ourselves in the story. We ask ourselves what we would do in the situation, calling on our own ideas and experience and making the story something we can relate to. That's why storytelling creates changes of opinion and knowledge that lasts.

As a leader, you can tell stories to illustrate desired behaviours, explain your values, share a lesson, clarify your strategic goals or describe a vision. Storytelling has so many benefits. Firstly, stories build trust. Your stories reveal who you are and your personality. They connect you with your people, transmitting information and your personal experience. Secondly, they can be used to convey concepts or ideas that might otherwise be difficult to articulate, such as a complicated process.

Most importantly, stories inspire others to act. Leaders are often concerned about *what* they want to tell people or *how* they want to tell people something. But your first question should be, "How do I want to make them feel?" Stories that evoke imagination and emotion can be highly persuasive. We remember what we feel.

And, let's face it, stories are fun. Would you rather tell someone what to do or show them through a story? Telling people is not motivating. But a story that makes people join the dots and experience that real "a-ha" moment is powerful. By allowing your people to unpack the story themselves, you make a lasting impact. You pull people in rather than push your message, and you invite them to come along for the journey and participate.

IDEAS FOR EFFECTIVE STORYTELLING:

- **Check your intention for telling a story.** Do you want to reveal a genuine part of yourself, build trust, connect people, share a lesson learnt or impart knowledge? (All great reasons). Or do you want to manipulate others or make yourself look good? If that's the case, you might end up doing the opposite.

- **Bring your story to life by evoking all the senses.** What did you see, hear, feel, smell and taste? Immerse your people in the experience and paint a picture. Take them on a journey. In *The Hero with a Thousand Faces*, author Joseph Campbell describes the idea of a monomyth, an archetypal narrative structure that describes the hero's journey. The hero's journey starts with an ordinary person who experiences a call to adventure. Then there is a three-part structure comprised of the departure or challenge, the action and transformation, and finally the return. This structure gives stories a simple yet powerful framework. Each story needs conflict and resolution, tension and release, mystery and revelation. There must be losses and triumphs, peaks and troughs.

- **Take time to craft your stories and practice them.** Make them compelling. I always giggle when people hear a speaker and say what a wonderful, natural storyteller they are. Of course, they might be a natural, but chances are they have also spent a lot of time and energy crafting and practising the right delivery. They have received feedback on their stories and reworked them.

- **Ensure there is simplicity in your story.** Choose your words carefully. No one wants a long-winded version. There is an art to including just enough detail to set the scene and evoke emotion without cluttering your story and losing your audience. Every sentence must add to the story.

- **Take care to select the right story.** Tell it at the right time to the right audience. Stories about failing and learning from your mistakes pull people in. Stories that serve only to self-promote turn people away.

- **Tell the truth, the whole truth.** If you leave the bad bits out of the story, you build distrust. You need to be vulnerable with your storytelling and have the courage to tell your truth. It's the pain people will learn from the most.

- **Make your stories relatable.** People want to feel you have experienced their problems, pain and fear. They also want to know how you overcame them. Stories that feel familiar – "I've been there, too" – are the most powerful because they're relatable. The audience can imagine themselves in the story, being the hero of their own journey, and are more likely to connect with and remember what you're saying.

Stories make us more alive,
more human, more courageous,
more loving.

MADELEINE L'ENGLE

A FINAL
MESSAGE

A Final Message

The legal profession in this time of disruption and uncertainty needs lawyers, like you, who will lead with conviction and confidence. Rapid advancements in technology mean the practice of law will continue to evolve. In the market, the competition for both clients and talent is fierce. Only the law firms that embrace a new type of leadership – a leadership that is authentic, adaptable and highly collaborative – will emerge as market leaders.

You've focussed and worked hard on your legal skills, knowledge and expertise. Now, it's time to seize the opportunity to invest in your development as a leader and move into a position of influence. It's time to step out of your comfort zone and be adventurous, courageous and try something new.

The first step is to get your head in the leadership game and create an effective mindset to gain the confidence you need to lead others. Secondly, you must gain clarity on your new leadership

A FINAL MESSAGE

identity – who are you as a leader and what you stand for. Show yourself and be vulnerable. Let your people see the real you. And finally, the third step is to develop practical leadership skills to coach, motivate and inspire your people. All three steps are needed to become a leader people want to follow; a leader who builds connection and heartfelt commitment with their people.

As a legal leader, you inspire and influence others. You create a team that supports and challenges one another and works collaboratively to achieve exceptional results. You encourage the growth and development of your people. You show them their full potential.

You create the unwritten ground rules in your team and your people look to you for direction and inspiration. This is why I believe leadership is an absolute privilege and a role you either commit to 100% or leave to someone who will.

So, are you up for the challenge? I think you are.

It's time to transform from Great Lawyer to Great Leader!

Want More?

Midja FISHER

Midja is an authentic, engaging and powerful speaker, mentor and facilitator. She delivers corporate leadership and culture programs with high impact and energy. Her programs create lasting change and sustainable outcomes for her clients.

There are a number of ways you can connect and work with Midja:

1. Book Midja to speak at your next conference or event.
2. Ask her to facilitate the Great Lawyer to Great Leader program in your firm.
3. Join Midja's Women with Confidence mentoring program.
4. Subscribe to Midja's weekly video blog, "Mondays with Midja".
5. Follow, like and share.

LINKEDIN
www.linkedin.com/in/midja/

FACEBOOK
www.facebook.com/midja.leadership

INSTAGRAM
www.instagram.com/midja_fisher/

www.midja.com.au
midja@midja.com.au
0408 718 445